Eazy PMP

AITechConsulting

To order additional copies of this book, contact:
Xlibris Corporation
1-888-795-4274
www.Xlibris.com
Orders@Xlibris.com
101434

Contents

This concise book is written for the following purposes:

- Project Management Professionals,
- PMP Certification exam preparation,
- Last-minute project management exam revision,
- Project Management first timers.

This revision note was put together in close collaboration with successful program and project managers, business owners, consultants, entrepreneurs, and students with the objective of presenting concise and accurate information on project management in less than one hundred pages for rapid learning.

AITechConsulting

Dedication

This book is dedicated to my family, friends, and readers that are wishing me the best and success in my next journey of life.

Preface

As a professional engineer, businessperson, project manager, consultant, program manager, and most especially a student forever (continuously learning based on projects and operation scenarios), I have put together this minibook on project management to help those in the pursuit of becoming a project management professional. I attained my certification exam based on work experience and self-learning of the PMBOK guide. That is, the study of *Project Management Body of Knowledge (PMBOK Guide),* **fourth edition. I did study other project management books such as the following:**

1. *PMP Exam Prep, Sixth Edition: Rita's Course in a Book for Passing the PMP Exam*
2. *The PMP Exam: How to Pass on Your First Try*, **fourth edition by Andy Crowe**
3. "Tips on PMP Exam" by Jim Owens

Remember, I said self-learning. This is to save cost and maximize the use of my self-initiative and drive. If I can do it, you can also do it.

This minibook is an expansion of what I learnt and revised weeks before the exam to help me consolidate my knowledge on PMP topics for passing the exam. The consolidation of knowledge after reading different books, articles, and practicing knowledge gained on program management and system engineering experience enabled me to obtain my PMP certification. I wish you the best of luck as you read through this minibook to aid your knowledge and move you closer to passing your PMP certification.

"PMI," "PMP," "Project Management Professional," and "PMBOK" are registered certification marks of the Project Management Institute (PMI) Inc. in the United States and other nations. This is nonprofit organization helping to drive industry best practices in project management.

Although the author has made every effort to ensure accuracy and completeness of information contained in this book, he can assume no responsibility for errors, inaccuracies, omissions, or inconsistencies contained herein.

Chapter 1: Preparing for PMP exam

Thinking about taking a PMP (Project Management Professional) exam? This is a good place to start for information on the purpose of the exam, the makeup of the exam, and where to get more information:

1. The purpose of the exam is to test your general understanding, analysis, and knowledge application of project management.
2. There are two hundred questions in the exam—only one hundred seventy-five of the questions count toward pass/fail score on the exam. *One hundred thirty-five* of the questions must be passed (68.5 percent). The other twenty-five questions are experimental questions. You will not be able to identify these questions in the exam. Answer as many questions as possible correctly.
3. The exam contains multiple-choice questions. Choose from four answers.
4. Pick the most appropriate answers from the four choices. When there are more than one likely answer, look for the answer that favors the customer.
5. The exams changes every time you take it. There are no two PMP exams that are the same because they are randomly selected from a large database of questions.
6. The time to complete the exam is four hours. It flies quickly if you are well prepared.
7. Practice as many questions as you can from a wide range of selections from books, articles, and the Internet.
8. The Project Management Institute (PMI) is the not-for-profit membership association coordinating the standards for project management profession. Visit *www.pmi.org* for more information.

9. There is a fee for taking PMP exam. Visit *www.pmi.org* for details of payment and renewing your certification when you have passed the exam.
10. You can also download a copy of the EazyPMP training software at *www.eazypmp.com* to speed up you pace in learning this material. The software has both audio and text to aid your learning of this book.
11. Mobile application of EazyPMP is also available in Google market for mobile applications and on www.eazypmp.com.

Good luck.

Chapter 2: About the PMP Exam

The PMP examination questions are designed to test your aptitude in the following areas:

1. Knowledge,
2. Application, and
3. Analysis.

The following table is a description of the allocation of the PMP exam. This may change as PMI revises the PMP exam, but you can use the table as a general guideline because variation for the values will not be drastically different:

Process Group	Number of Questions	% of Exam
Initiating	23	11.5%
Planning	46	23%
Executing	53	26.5%
Monitoring and Controlling	42	21%
Closing	18	9%
Professional and Social Responsibility	18	9%

The key is to know your material. You will be tested on every process group and the knowledge areas of the process group.

Chapter 3: On the Day of the Exam

Take the following items with you to the exam center:

1. The PMP exam eligibility letter.
2. Two pieces of identification (for example, driver's license and passport were acceptable).
3. A nonprogrammable calculator. (This was provided on a computer-based exam center.)
4. Pencil/pen.
5. Snack and water. (You can take few minutes breaks between the exams.)
6. Dress appropriately for the environment and weather.
7. Stay calm, relax, take your time, but you only have four hours.

Other ideas that you should keep in mind to aid in passing PMP exam:

1. Think PMBOK/PMI all the time when answering the questions—not your ways but PMBOK/PMI.
2. Memorization is not enough to pass the exam but an understanding of the process group and the functional areas.
3. Use the paper provided for your calculations and to brain dump formulas memorized for the exam.
4. Answer the easy questions first, then tackle the harder ones afterward. All questions carry equal marks. One point per question. You need to answer at least 160 questions; twenty-five of the questions answered may not count because they are experimental questions, and 135 questions *must be* answered correctly to pass. Increase your chances of passing by attempting all two hundred questions.

5. Look for best the answer. Eliminate the wrong answer first then select the correct answers.
6. Prepare for calculations for Network Analysis and Earned Value.
7. For USA based questions on ethics, Proactive Management Approach the PMBOK way is the most correct answer.

Chapter 4: Project

The project management team is responsible for determining what practice is good for any given project. There are similarities between projects and operations. This section highlights on what is a *project* and its differences from *operations*.

What is a project?

The following diagram shows a project phased out into iterations. Each of the iterations is a complete project

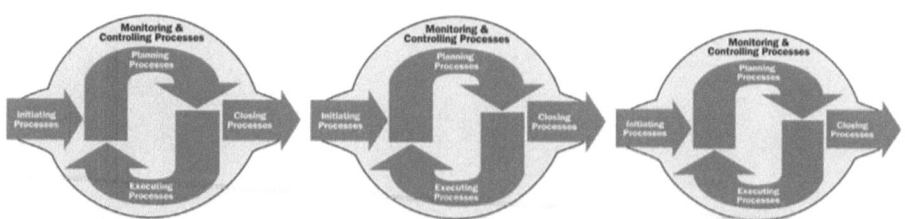

Figure 1. Project Iterations

The following are the characteristics of a project:

- A project is a *temporary* endeavor to create a product, service, or result.
- It has a defined purpose and may be in phases.
- It has a *definite* begin-and-end dates.
- It has a *finite* duration. (The duration may be short or long.)
- It may have social, economical, or environmental impacts.
- It creates *unique* deliverables (products, services, or results).

- A project's complete scope may not be understood at the beginning. The following approach is used to eventually gain full understanding and execution of a project:
  - *Rolling Wave Planning* and *Progressive Elaboration*
    - Developing the project in steps and continuing by increments.
    - A form of iterative waterfall approach with feedback.
    - Projects may change title as it progresses.
- A project must be delivered to the original purpose, changes must be phased, and all assets (resources) must be returned to the corporate pool at the end of the project.

What are the differences between project and operations?

Project	Operations
Project has a finite duration.	Operation is an ongoing and repetitive process.
Project is unique and temporary. It is terminated at the end of its objectives.	Operation is adaptive to new business objectives.
Project is a means of achieving strategic plan.	Operation is a means of continuing the execution of a work plan.

Projects are for strategic achievements

Projects are generally used as a means of achieving an organization strategic plan. The project team may be the employee of an organization or contracted service provider. The common strategic considerations or business drivers for project include the following:

- Market demands (e.g., the introduction of a new product into the market).
- Organization or business needs (e.g., the need for business process reengineering to improve daily operations).
- Technological advancement (e.g., the development of high-speed train for improved traveling time).

- Customer request (e.g., a customer request to build an estate of apartments).
- Legal requirements (e.g., the conversion of medical records to electronics document as mandated by federal government [EMR]).

Factors that contribute to successful projects

1. A *Well-Defined Scope*. Project scope must be clearly defined with a purpose.
2. *Sponsor*. The sponsor must have the need, power, and funding.
3. *Budget*. There is money available for the project.
4. *Will to Succeed*. Driven by the sponsor and aided by the project manager.
5. *Approval*. There must be buy in from sponsor and/or senior management.

Chapter 5: What is Project Management?

Project Management—Is the application of knowledge, skills, tools, and technique/method to deliver projects on time, on budget, and to specification (or project scope). The project management team is responsible for determining what practice is good for any given project. Whatever practice is chosen for the project, the project managers must be conscious of the triple constraints, and the integrated processes must be applied accordingly.

Triple Constraints—A project quality is defined by the triple constraints:

1. Project scope,
2. Time, and
3. Cost

Integrated Process Group—The process groups must be applied across the project:

- Initiating
- Planning
- Execution
- Monitor and Controlling
- Closing

Management by Projects—A number of organizations are adopting management by projects, structuring some of their operations into projects, but not all their operations.

Knowledge and skills required for project management

The practice of project management requires the understanding and the use of the following subject areas:

Project Management Body of Knowledge (PMBOK)—This is a book that is published by the Project Management Institute (PMI). It presents a set of standardized terminologies and guidelines that are generally accepted as project management information and practices. Visit *www.pmi.org* on how to obtain a copy for your study and project management practice. The PMBOK is organized into three sections:

1. The project management framework
    a. Organization or project environment
        i.   Social, economic, and cultural environment
        ii. Physical environment
        iii. Intellectual and political environment
    b. Project life cycle

2. The standard for project management practice. These are the five project management process groups:
    a. Initiating
    b. Planning
    c. Execution
    d. Monitor and control
    e. Closing

3. The project management knowledge areas
    a. Scope
    b. Time
    c. Cost
    d. Quality
    e. Human resources
    f. Communication
    g. Risk
    h. Procurement
    i. Fully integrated process of the above eight areas

Standard—This is a documented process established by consensus and approved by a regulated body for repeated use and guidelines.

Regulation—A government-imposed requirement. It is a mandatory compliance. A project may have to be executed under the guidance or restriction of government regulations. Project managers are expected to understand the project environment and comply with the regulations.

General Management Knowledge and Skills—These are general knowledge and skills required for project management:

- Financial management
- Purchasing and procurement
- Sales and marketing
- Strategic planning
- Health and safety
- Contract and law
- Manufacturing and distribution
- Logistics and supply chain
- Information technology

Portfolio Management—This is the management of collection of projects and programs that may be related or may not be related or inter-related. The following are some of the characteristics of a portfolio:

- Not interdependent.
- Portfolios are managed based on specific goals.
- Efficient use of resources.
- Managed by senior management.

Program Management—This is the management of a collection of related projects. There is the Program Management Office (PMO) associated with program management. The PMO helps to identify strategic key methods, standards, and tools for project managers to follow in managing and delivering key strategic initiatives (i.e., projects) while sharing information and documentation.

Subproject—Large projects may be divided into manageable components to easy project management.

Chapter 6: What is Project Life Cycle?

In organizations, every project and the management of the project are in the context of the processes, tools, and techniques appropriate and applicable to the organization. Project life cycle is a representation of the phases that connect the projects from the beginning to the end. The following diagram shows the relationship between project life cycle and project process group. Study the diagram and phase a project to gain an understanding of how it applies to organizations:

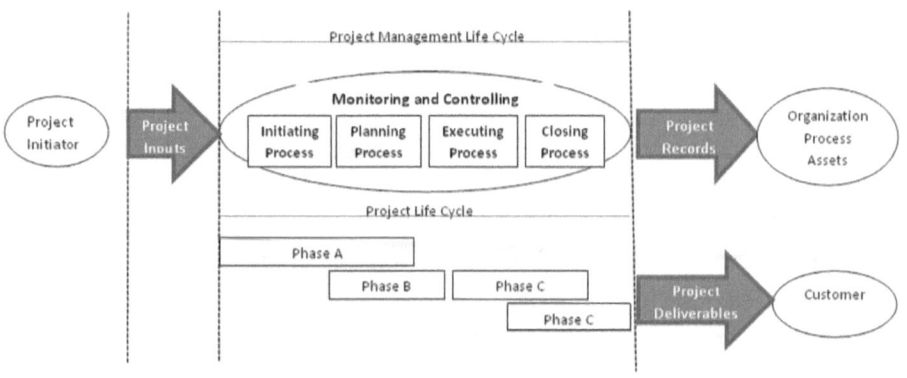

The following are some of the terms associated with project life cycle:

- **Project Management**—Provides the oversight to ensure that the project is delivered on time, on budget, to specification.
- **Project Processes**—These are steps to be undertaken by the project team in each phase of the project. The following are some of the steps that are common in the engineering field that may be applicable in other industries:

- ○ **System Implementation**
  - ▪ Analysis
  - ▪ Design
  - ▪ Development
  - ▪ Implementation
- ○ **Rational Unified Process (RUP)**
  - ▪ Inception
  - ▪ Elaboration
  - ▪ Construction
  - ▪ Transition

What is the project process in your organization?

- • **Project Delivery**—This is the execution of tasks defined for the steps in the project phases. These tasks are undertaken by the project team to fulfill the project requirement.
- • **Deliverables**—These are the outputs of the tasks defined in the project delivery.
- • **Schedule Compression**
  - ○ **Fast Tracking**—Reordering the sequence of activities in project phases so that next phase begins before the deliverable of the current phase. Activities are performed in parallel.
  - ○ **Crashing**—This is the adding of more resources to project activity so that it can be completed quickly.

Chapter 7: Project Stakeholders and Organization

Who are the project stakeholders?

Project stakeholders are individuals and organizations that are actively involved in the project or whose interest may be affected as a result of the project execution or completion. The following are some of the stakeholders on a given project:

- Individuals, organizations, or customers
- Project team
- Provider of financial (or sponsor) and political support
- Influencer—Influences project managers' decisions for desirable outcomes
- Benefits positively from the project—Positive stakeholders (e.g., oil refinery)
- Negative stakeholders—See negative outcomes from the project (e.g., location of oil refinery)
- Program Management Office (PMO)—Coordinators of project management standards, assets, and templates

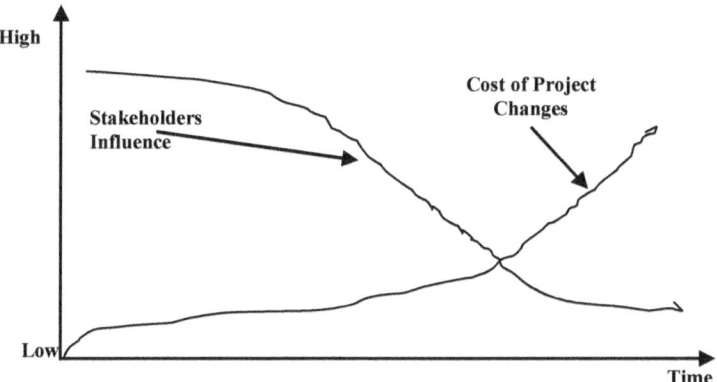

Figure 2. Stakeholders' Influence and Cost of Change

Organizational Structure and Project Organization

It is important for project managers to understand the organizational structure and framework in which they are going to manage projects. The following questions must be answered for the project to be undertaken by a project manager:

What is the organizational structure for this project?

Is the organization project focused? To fully understand and answer the organizational structure for a project, the project manager should investigate the response to the following questions:

- **Framework**
  - What is the project organization?
  - Who do you report to?
  - Is matrix organization?
  - What is the power and authority of the project manager?
  - Is this a project-driven organization?
  - Is this a hierarchical organization?
  - Who is the project sponsor?
  - Who does the sponsor report to?

- **Structure**
  - How does a project get delivered?
  - How does a project get initiated or accepted?
- **Culture**
  - What is the organization's culture?
  - Do they value people?
  - Must everything be done at all cost?

What is the organizational framework?

Most projects are executed within an organization with a framework in place that guides the overall operation of the organization. It is very important that the project manager understands the organizational framework to manage a project effectively within an organization. The following questions should help to investigate the organizational framework:

- **Structural-Organization Chart**
  - Who reports to whom?
  - Who has the power to ensure that the project gets delivered successfully?
- **Human Resources**
  - How are employees treated?
  - Do the employees come first or project comes first?
  - What is the work ethics? Is forty hours per week or overtime expected?
  - Are the organization people driven?
  - What is the attitude to training?
  - Is there on-the-job training?
  - Is the project the most important?
- **Political Framework**
  - **Internal Politics**—Who must be happy to ensure that your project is successful?
  - Who has the power?
  - **External Politics**—Who do you have to work with externally to ensure the project is successful?
  - Who is your ally?
- **Symbolic**
  - What is the dress code?
  - Is the boss approachable?

- o   Is this a hierarchy organization?
- o   Is this a formal or friendly environment?
- o   What is the norm?

Organizational Structure

The type of organizational structure surrounding a project often determines how resources are managed and their availability for projects. Power and authority will be determined by the organizational structure. The organizational structure also helps to answer most of the questions posed in previous sections. The following are the types of organizational structure applicable in various organizations:

Functional Organization

- •   This is a traditional business organization where you have the head, the CEO (Chief Executive Officer), broken down into the appropriate business/functional areas with the respective VP, managers, and functional area owners.

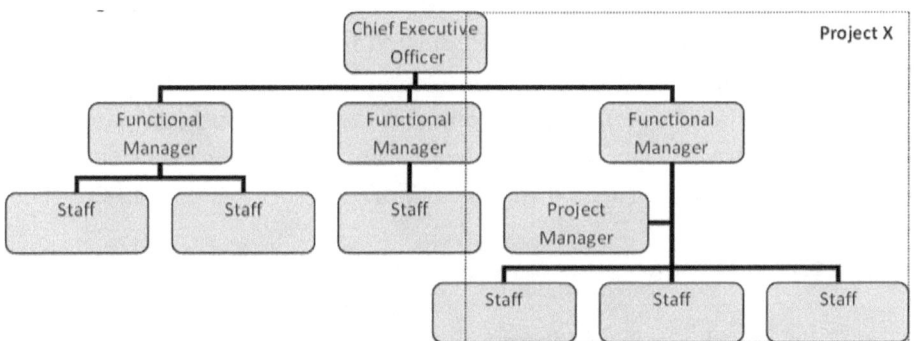

Figure 3. Functional Organization

- •   Project is delivered within the business units.
- •   Project managers are also line managers who have other responsibilities other than the projects.
- •   Team members are from the same business units as indicated by the box labeled Project *X.*

Projectized Organization

The characteristics of a projectized organization include the following:

- Organization is focused mainly on projects, no other responsibilities.
- Project-based organization—The organization is project based and has a head with project managers leading the project areas and reporting to the head. The team members report to the project managers.
- The project managers have high to almost total authority.

Figure 4. Projectized Organization

- The resources available are dedicated to the project.
- The project manager controls the budget.
- This type of organization is common to consulting companies that mainly focus on project delivery. This project organization does not exist in traditional organizations.

Matrix Organization

- This is the most common form of organization, a combination of the traditional functional business organization and the project organization.
- Cross-functional business areas determined by engagements or projects.
- There are three types:
  - **Weak Matrix**—Project for a business unit is executed by team members from multiple business units as indicated by the shaded area. *Advantage:* Special skills and knowledge can be pulled from various business units of the organization for the success of the project. *Disadvantage:* The team members still have to report to

their line managers. There may be conflicts between objectives of the project manager and the line managers of the various team members. The project manager assumes a coordinator role, minimal authority, and control on resources.

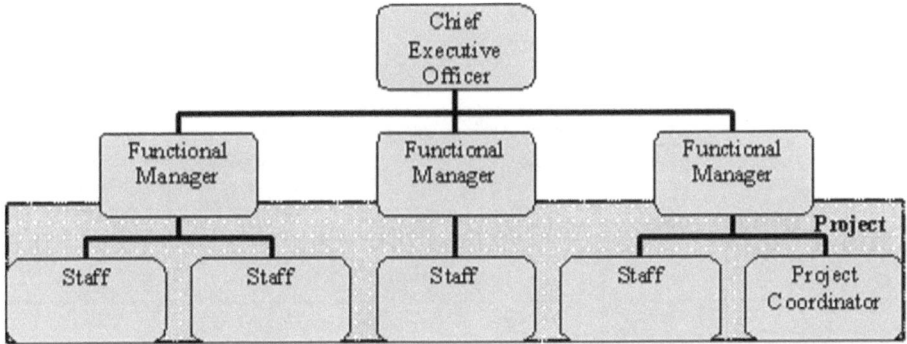

Figure 5. Weak Matrix Organization

- o **Balanced Matrix**—Similar to weak matrix organization with the exception of providing a dedicated project manager with considerable authority and full-time administrative staffs.
- o **Strong Matrix**—Strong projectized organization characteristics but with limitations imposed by functional organization. *Advantage:* Special skills and knowledge can be pulled from various business units of the organization for the success of the project. Dedicated project managers and administrative staffs. *Disadvantage:* the team members still have to report to their line managers. There may be conflicts between objectives of the project manager and the line managers of the various team members.

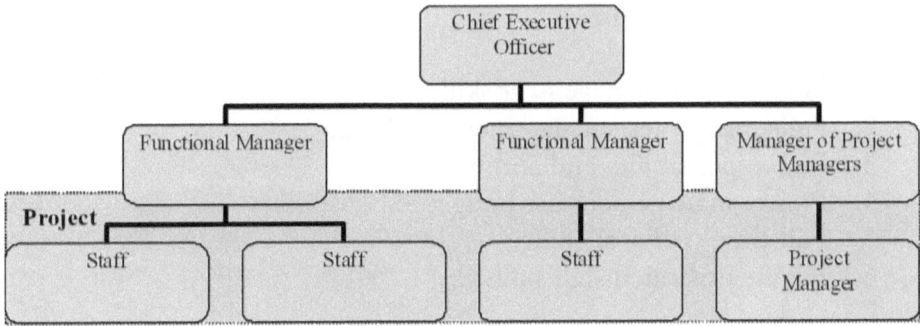

Figure 6. Strong Matrix Organization

Composite Organization

- This type of organization combines all the various types of organizational structures.
- A department may have its dedicated project team.

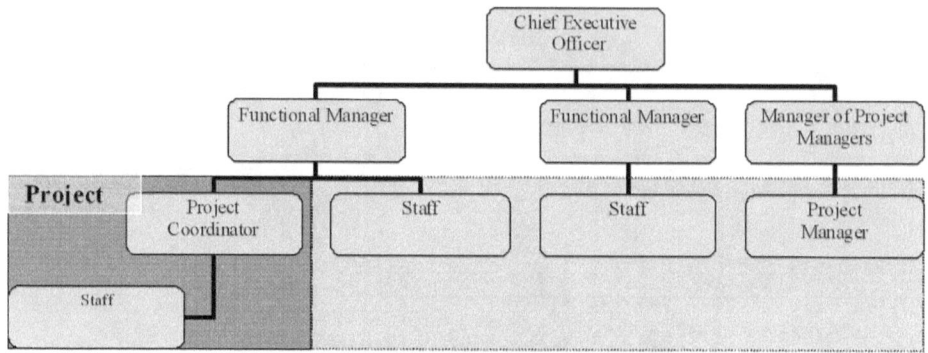

Figure 7. Composite Organization

Comparison of the Organizational Structure by Project Manager Skills

Functional Organization

1. Limited project management skills.
2. Part-time project management availability.
3. Wide range of authority. High degree of authority over team members.
4. Functional manager has the budget ownership.
5. Staff availability is part-time.
6. Wide range of staff skills.

Projectized Organization

1. High project management skills.
2. Full-time project management availability.
3. Full responsibility and authority.
4. Project management has budget responsibility.
5. Full-time staff availability.
6. Highly dedicated staff skills.

Weak Matrix Organization

1. Limited project management skills.
2. Part-time project management availability.
3. Low authority over team members.
4. Functional manager has the budget ownership.
5. Staff availability is part-time.
6. Wide range of staff skills.

Strong Matrix Organization

1. High project management skills.
2. Full-time project management availability.
3. Medium authority over team members.
4. Project manager has the budget ownership.
5. Staff availability is part-time and full-time.
6. Wide range of staff skills.

What is the organizational culture?

Organization culture is an important environment factor that also contributes to the success of a project. Project managers should make attempts to answer the following questions in determining the culture that surrounds their projects. The answers to these questions will help them to make effective decisions that will aid the success of their projects:

1. What is the corporate identity of the organization? Leader, follower, or innovative?
2. What is the corporate versus individual emphasis? Do we focus more on profit (bottom line) or if the employees are happy? A profit or employee-driven organization or well balanced?
3. Business integration: Share or compete for budgets? Some organizations expect their business units to compete for the research and development money to push the overall success of the company.
4. Does the organization take risk? Risk tolerance? Does the organization believe that risky project will bring more success?
5. What is the organization focus? Long or short term? To be profitable in five years or in one year?

6. What is the overall company overall maturity? Startup, mature, or established company? This determines how project managers should operate the projects (project/product/company maturity). Is project management methodology well embraced in the organization? What is the project management methodology and project life cycle?

These factors determine how successful your project will be in the organization because they are the environments that support the project.

Other Supporting Systems and Office for Project Organization

Program Management Office (PMO)

The PMO serves the following functions to aid project success:
- Management of multiple projects enabling project template sharing.
- Provides advisory support on projects.
- Recommends policies and procedures where necessary.
- Provides administrative support to project managers.
- Serves a centralized management point for project managers.

Project Management System

The project management systems are the tools, techniques, methods, and procedures for managing projects.

Chapter 8: What is Project Management Process?

The *project management process* by PMI standards consist of processes recognized as good practice globally, and across industry groups, to enhance the chances of success over a wide range of project executions. The PM process ensures that we have the management in place *to support* the project process, and we have the management structure in place *to do* the project process.

The *project manager and team*, in collaboration, are always responsible for determining what processes are appropriate for any given project. The project management processes as defined in the PMBOK guide is a combination of the five process groups and the nine knowledge areas.

Other processes that may apply in project management depending on your industry include:

- Product-Oriented Process.
- Customer-Centric Process.
- Plan-Do-Check-Act Cycle—The project management process group is based on this principle.

The *project management process groups* per PMI standards are as follows:

- **Initiating**—Define and authorize the project phases. Is this a valid project? Should this project take place?
- **Planning**—Define and refine project objectives and scope to be achieved. We define the steps required for the schedule, project process, resources, budget planning. This defines how the project is done.

- **Executing**—Project delivery. The process integrates resources and people to carry out project objectives. The actual delivery of the project—a team member functions. The most hours and expenses are incurred during this phase.
- **Monitoring and Control**—This is an active process through the project life cycle executed by the project manager who regularly measures and monitors progress so that corrective actions can be taken when meaningful. The process ensures that we are on time and on budget and delivering to expectations.
- **Closing**—This is about gaining the final acceptance of the project. It brings the project to an orderly end.

Project Management Process versus Project Process

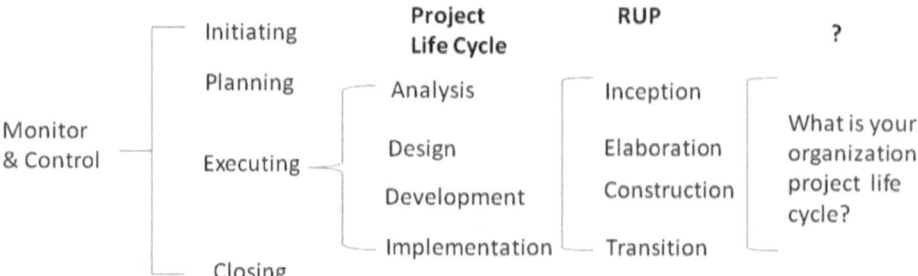

The execution of project life cycle takes place during the *execution process* of project management process groups. The project life cycle is determined by the project manager and team members of the project. They determine what project life cycle and the rigor of implementation in the execution phase. Every industry has its applicable project life cycle. What project life cycle is applicable to your organization?

Project Management: Level of Activity Chart (Time versus Effort)

The following chart is the level of activity over time in the project management process groups:

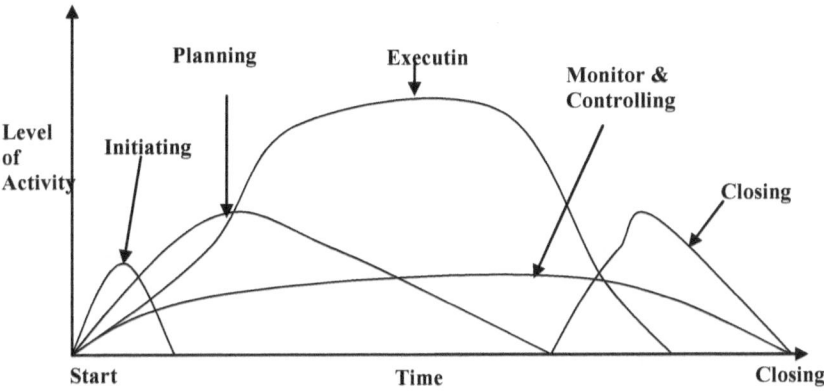

The following points should be noted for the level of activity chart and PM process groups:

- **Initiating**—An intense and short activity at the beginning of the project.
- **Planning**—Ramps up early at the beginning project and then levels of over the course of the project. The ramp is due to resource planning, project planning, and scope planning; all the initial planning takes place here. The continuation of planning on the chart is due to ongoing planning and re-planning required for keeping the project on track.
- **Executing**—Project execution starts slowly and ramps up over the life of the project. It falls toward the end of the project and has the most activities, that is, the delivery of the project (analysis, design development, and implementation).
- **Monitoring and Controlling**—As shown on the graph, this goes through the entire life of a project. It ensures that the project is on time, on budget, and according to specification.
- **Closing**—It brings the project to orderly close. Closing is generally brief and a fast process to bring the project into closure.

The process groups are executed once per project or once per phase of a project. They can be done at each phase of the project life cycle. The process groups are repeatable steps for each phase of the project life cycle. The phases of the project life cycle are dependent on the organizational industry standard, but for this purpose, we used analysis, design, development, and implementation.

Why iterate project management process groups?

Project iterations are necessary for large projects to breakdown projects into manageable processes. Traditional planning of engineering projects is organized around product or service breakdown and development as inherited from manufacturing and construction industries. Today and the future are about process breakdown into manageable and repeatable processes to produce different deliverables that ultimately result to the overall objective of the project. This approach of process breakdown at project management process groups and project life cycle (e.g., IBM, *In the Rational Unified Process [RUP]*) enables the following benefits:

1. To revalidate project for risk assessment and continuity of the project.
2. Re-planning as needed based on evaluation or revalidation.
3. Introduce improvement where necessary.

Chapter 9: Planning a Project from End to End Using PMBOK

The following table is an organization of the process group relative to the knowledge areas per project management processes from the fourth edition of the PMBOK guide:

Knowledge Areas	Process Group				
	Initiating	Planning	Executing	Monitor & Controlling	Closing
Integration	• Develop project charter	• Develop project management plan	• Direct and manage project execution	• Monitor & control project work • Perform integrated change control	• Close project or phase
Scope		• Collect requirements • Define scope • Create WBS		• Verify scope • Control scope	
Time		• Define activities • Sequence activities • Estimate activity resources • Estimate activity durations • Develop schedule		• Control schedule	
Cost		• Estimate costs • Determine budget		• Control costs	
Quality		• Plan quality	• Perform quality assurance	• Perform quality control	
Human Resource		• Develop human resource plan	• Acquire project team • Develop project team • Manage project team		

Communications	• Identify stakeholders	• Plan communications	• Distribute information • Manage stakeholder expectations	• Report performance	
Risk		• Plan risk management • Identify risks • Perform qualitative risk analysis • Perform quantitative risk analysis • Plan risk responses		• Monitor and control risks	
Procurement		• Plan procurement	• Conduct procurement	• Administer procurement	• Close procurements

Here are the steps to be followed with reference to the PMBOK table:

Initiating

Develop project charter. The project charter is needed to define the scope of the project and also gain the formal approval for the official start of a project.

Planning

Develop project management plan. This is a critical component of the project management process. A well-developed project management plan helps to guide the successful execution of the project.

Collect requirements. Using the project charter, the project manager and project team facilitate workshops and interviews, brainstorming exercise, and group activities to define the detailed scope for the project.

Define scope. All collected requirements and the overall project scope is agreed with the stakeholders.

Create WBS. Develop **work** **b**reakdown **s**tructure. Deliverables are broken down into manageable smaller tasks required to achieve the scope.

Define activities. This is a list of activities identified during the *Create WBS*—the list of activities to be executed to produce the deliverables defined for the scope of the project.

Sequence activities. In what order should the activities listed be executed? A project life cycle approach might help to achieve this process.

Estimate activity resources. Estimate the resources needed to carry out the activities defined for this project. Resources may include materials, human resources, building, hardware, and software. Basically, the resources needed to accomplish the execution of a successful project.

Estimate activity duration. Estimate the time required to execute the activities defined in previous process.

Develop schedule. Using all the activity information defined in previous steps, develop a schedule using available tool, for example, Microsoft Project software.

Estimate cost. Using time and the resources as parameters, determine the overall cost of the project.

Determine budget. Develop budget for estimated cost of resources, materials, services, and contracts needed for the project. The determined budget should include contingency plan in case of cost overrun.

Plan quality. Establish the quality standard required for the project to ensure that the project management process incorporates it. The "do it right the first time" principle and total quality management approach.

Develop human resources plan. Develop plan for resources, when resources are needed, and when they exit the project based on schedule, training process, team communication process, conflict resolutions, and effective teamwork.

Plan communications. Plan and define what information will be communicated and distributed on the project. Define how the information will be communicated on the project.

Plan risk management. Create a proactive risk management plan. The plan should include identified risks, risk analysis, and planned risk responses.

Identify risks. Create a list of possible risks on the project.

Perform qualitative risk analysis. Using expert judgment, experience, and probability, weigh identified risks; assign a level of prioritization; and rank them.

Perform quantitative risk analysis. Using expert judgment, experience, and probability, weigh identified risks by assigning a projected monetary value to each risk, and rank them.

Plan risk response. Using expert judgment, experience, and results from risk analysis, prepare proactive responses to the risks identified. These responses are guides for managing the risks.

Plan procurement. This is the planning of what to buy, how much to buy, and when to buy needed (materials, services, and contracts) resources for the project.

Executing

Direct and manage project execution. This is the process where the project manager and project team perform actions to execute the project management plan. The project management team directs the performance of the project activities and manages the interfaces of the project organization.

Perform quality assurance. This is the continuous improvement process for the project. Improve and correct deficiencies as part of the project life cycle, analyze and audit process, recommend corrective actions, improve standards and processes. The update the project management planned accordingly.

Develop project team. Build the project team by colocation (war room), training, team building exercise, recognition and reward, setting ground rules, and team performance assessment.

Manage project team. Manage the project team by observing performance, monitoring issues, resolving conflicts, and completing performance appraisals.

Distribute information. Using the defined list in the communication management plan, distribute project information to the respective stakeholders using the predefined models and methods.

Manage stakeholder expectations. Stakeholders' expectations on the project must be continuously managed and met via effective communication of any changes on the project.

Conduct procurement. This is the execution of the activities defined in the procurement management plan. These activities include short listing qualified vendors or sellers, evaluating seller proposals, conducting bidder conferences, selecting sellers, and awarding procurement contract.

Monitoring and Controlling

Monitor and control project work. This process is performed to measure the project deliverables and the process by which they are produced against the planned processes and standards defined in the project management plan.

Perform integrated change control. All the needed or requested changes in the project must be assessed for impact analysis on the project. This is the control process that enables the project team to evaluate the acceptability of a change for execution.

Verify scope. Scope verification is ensuring that the deliverables from the project meet the documented scope. Gold plating is not allowed and neither should the project team underdeliver to the project scope. The formal acceptance of stakeholders on project deliverables takes place during this process.

Control scope. Controlling the scope of the project is ensuring that change requests are within project scope. Any change request outside the project scope is channeled through the *Perform integrated change control* process.

Control schedule. This is part of the perform-integrated change control to monitor schedule changes and the factors influencing the changes.

Control cost. Monitor cost changes, factors contributing to the changes, preventing cost overrun, monitor cost performance and variances from baseline.

Perform quality control. The monitoring of project product and deliverables and their conformance to relevant quality standards.

Report performance. This is the collection and distribution of project performance information. This information include status reports, forecasting, and progress (per schedule) measurement.

Monitor and control risks. This is the tracking of risk identified in the project, identifying new risks, and executing the corresponding risk response plan defined in the project management plan.

Administer procurement. This process involves managing contracts between the seller of services or materials to the project and project management team. All deliverables and work performed are reviewed against the content of the contract. If any change to the contract, the appropriate contract change control system is applied.

Closing

Close project or phase. This is the process of closing the project or phase of the project in an organized manner. Lesson learned is captured, contract closure is collaborated with the respective vendors, and all organization assets are updated with project documentation, forming part of historical information.

Close procurements. This is the formal closure of the contracts with the vendors or suppliers. All deliverables and product(s) are verified for acceptance, and contracts are terminated as needed, ideally, amicably.

Now that we have defined our approach for all the activities of the process groups for the end-to-end planning of the project, we need to expand on how we tackle each process and integrate them together for the success of the project. The following sections describe the knowledge areas and expand on the approach for each process in the process group.

Chapter 10: Integration Management

The project integration management knowledge area enables the project manager to have a high-level view of the project from start to finish. This should be the starting point when landed with a project engagement. Note the following project management processes and expand each process in a PMI compliant manner:

- Develop project charter.
- Develop project management plan.
- Direct and manage project execution.
- Monitor and control project work.
- Perform integrated change control.
- Close project or phase.

The following sections describe the listed project management processes and highlight the work to be carried in each process.

Develop Project Charter

The project charter is first deliverable from initiation phase, which officially indicates the start of a project. It is a high-level one—or two-page document that broadly describes the project.

The project charter covers the following:

- **Introduction into the project**—Description of the problems as described in the Statement of Work (SOW) issued for the project.

- **Business Objective**—This is the main component and *must be developed with the business sponsor(s)*. Business cases to be considered for this factor includes the following:

  - Market demand
  - Customer request
  - Legal requirement
  - Social need
  - Business needs
  - Technological advancement
  - Ecological requirement

- **Preliminary Cost/Benefit**—What are the benefits for this project? These benefits are needed to sell the project to the senior management and sponsor. What is the payback period on this project? To determine the cost and benefits, consider the following *project selection method*:

  - **Benefit Measurement Method**—Monetary benefit and cost
  - **Constraint Optimization**—Mathematical/calculus calculation
  - **Benefit Cost Ratio (BCR)**—If greater than 1 (one), good benefit over the cost. Project product sold more for the cost of the project (BCR = Selling price/cost price)
  - **Economic Value Add (EVA)**—The value created by project for its stakeholders. Keep the money in the bank if the return on project will be of a lesser value.
  - **Internal Rate of Return (IRR)**—Project return as interest. The bigger the return, the better the project.
  - **Net Present Value**—How much is the product of the project worth right now with the cost of the project taken out of the worth value? The bigger, the better.
  - **Present Value**—How much is the product of the project worth right now? The bigger, the better.
  - **Opportunity Cost**—What is the cost of the other opportunities we missed by investing our money in this project? Do not miss big opportunities. We can miss out on the smaller opportunity.
  - **Payback Period**—The quicker it takes to recover the investment on a project, the better. A shorter payback period is better than a longer one.
  - **Return on Investment (ROI)**—What percentage of return is made by investing on a project? Bigger is better.
  - **Return on Investment (ROIC)**—This is a measurement of how much is the return on every dollar spent on a project. Bigger is better.

- On completion of the project charter, a *formal approval* must be documented confirming the acceptance of the project to officially take place. The business sponsor, project manager, and senior management should all be in agreement on the content of the project charter and its feasibility.

Develop Project Management Plan

On receiving the approval of the project charter, the work required to complete the project must be planned. The project management plan document must be developed because it outlines briefly or in detail how the project is managed, executed, and controlled. This is more like a project guide.

Per PMI, the project management plan is expected to contain the description on the following headings:

- **Scope Management Plan**—The management and control of project scope.
- **Schedule Management Plan**—The management of project schedule.
- **Cost Management Plan**—The management of project cost, money allocation, and sourcing of funding.
- **Quality Management Plan**—The management of planning, assurance, and control on the project.
- **Process Improvement Plan**—The management of continuous improvement from the "plan, do, check, act" cycle or quality wheel feedback implementation on the project.
- **Human Resource Plan**—The administration and behavior management of project resources.
- **Communication Management Plan**—The management of planning, formation, and distribution of information on the project.
- **Risk Management Plan**—The management of planning, identification, analysis, monitor, and control of risk.
- **Procurement Management Plan**—The management of purchases of products and services needed from vendors to perform project work.
- **Schedule Baseline**—The original plan plus all approved changes. Approval by customer, sponsor, and the project manager.
- **Cost Performance Baseline**—The original plan cost plus all approved changes. Approval by customer, sponsor, and the project manager.

- **Scope Baseline**—The original scope plus all approved changes. Approval by customer, sponsor, and the project manager.
- **Change Management Plan**—The management of change process on the project.
- **Configuration Management Plan**—The management of identification, changes, storage, and status reporting on project deliverables.
- **Requirement Management Plan**—The management of activities required to gather, handle changes, decide, and document requirements.

The listed headings do not have to be in a single document; they can be separated into their own documents depending on the scale of the project and how detailed the plan is required.

Direct and Manage Project Execution

In direct and manage project execution, the project manager spends most of the time managing resources, cost, and time. The team members are executing the work packages and creating deliverables. The project manager integrates the team and work using the project management plan to create the project deliverables, change request, and/or corrective actions. The project management plan is the master plan.

Monitor and Control Project Work

- The project manager continuously measures the project execution and deliverables against expectations as defined in the project management plan. He/she makes decisions based on results to ensure that the project is going according to plan. Specific areas of measurement by the project manager include project schedule, project information and distribution, issues and risks, resource performance, project performance, and procurement process.

Perform Integrated Change Control

- Project managers are expected to have a structured method of managing change in project because change is inevitable in every project. The perform integrated change control ensures that all changes requested or needed on the project are evaluated for their impact on the project. An impact analysis on the various sections of the project management plan is carried out to ensure success of the project. The output of this process includes: approved change request and requested change request.

All change requests feed directly into direct and manage project execution process.

Close Project or Phase

This process guides the project manager in shutting down a project in an orderly manner. The key tasks for this process include the following:

- Create documentation and archive.
- Capture lesson learned.
- Close contract.
- Update organization assets (including historical project portfolio).
- Recover organization assets.

Chapter 11: Scope Management

This is the management of defining all the work required to complete the project. Inclusive in this knowledge area is ensuring that only the work required for the project is executed to expectations. The project scope must be clearly and well defined and communicated to the stakeholders. The following are the activities to be managed under scope management:

- **Collect Requirements**
  - Facilitate requirement-gathering workshops.
  - Refine requirements.
  - Document requirements.
- **Define Scope**
  - Determine project scope statement based on the collected requirements.
- **Create Work Breakdown Structure**
  - A top-down decomposition of deliverables to create the project work required and subdivided into manageable smaller components for project management.
- **Verify Scope**
  - Work with the stakeholders to ensure they approve the scope of the project.
  - Ensure and plan a formal acceptance of each deliverable to obtain sign off.
  - Establish a timeline for the review and feedback. Client needs to have a specified timeline to come back with feedback.
  - Turn around. Insist on a single set of comments. A formal acceptor must provide the feedback or comments to avoid conflicting comments.
  - Interim acceptance process must be established.

- ▪ Put an acceptance process in place by section of the deliverable document.
    - For example, Section 1 is accepted and no further changes are required.
    - Section 2 is still open for changes. There are minor changes to be added before acceptance.
  - ○ Resubmit
- **Scope Control**
  - ○ Manage change. Establish a process to manage the project scope and the needed changes. (Change management.)
  - ○ Integrate change:
    - Schedule team
    - Risk
  - ○ Establish a formal acceptance to the project scope changes.

Expected Outputs

The expected output from scope management knowledge area when executed per PMP standard includes the following:

- Project scope statement
  - ○ Work breakdown structure (WBS) with work package identifier, control account, work packages, unique account identification, cost summation, schedule summation, and resource information.
  - ○ WBS Dictionary with work package identifier, work package description, account codes, cost estimation, control account, milestone list, list of resources, statement of work, and responsible organization.
- Scope Baseline = Scope Statement + WBS + WBS Dictionary. This is an important output that feeds into the following processes:
  - ○ Control scope.
  - ○ Define activities.
  - ○ Estimate costs.
  - ○ Determine budget.
  - ○ Plan quality.
  - ○ Identify risks.
  - ○ Plan procurement.
- Scope Management Plan
- Requested Changes—These are not necessarily approved changes.

Chapter 12: Time Management

The project time management is a knowledge area that covers the definition of activities, resource estimating, and the development of schedule processes to be managed by the project manager. The *primary input* for executing the processes defined for time management is the *scope baseline*. The scope baseline is inclusive of scope statement, work breakdown structure, and the work breakdown dictionary. The processes for project time management and what they entail are as follows:

- **Define Activities**
    - Document the work to be performed.
    - Define activities base on work and schedule, *not* on deliverables.
    - Further decompose the work defined in the Work Breakdown Structure (WBS) into activities.
    - Decompose one Work Breakdown Structure (WBS) to one resource.
    - Apply *Rolling Wave Planning*. Develop detailed activities and assign corresponding time frame. It provides a certain degree of time estimation accurate enough to plan the project or next phase. The following table is an example of rolling wave planning:

Activity	Deliverable	Work/Schedule
Analysis	DLV 1	Time 1 (20 days)
Design	DLV 2 DLV 3	Time 2 (30 days) Time 3 (40 days)

Development	DLV 4	Time 4 (40 days)
Project Management	DLV 5	Time 5 (150 days)

- **Sequence Activities**
  - Define the sequencing between the tasks.
  - Define the type of dependencies:
    - Finish to start
    - Finish to finish
    - Start to start
  - Focus on the mandatory dependencies; this may include optional dependencies but may bring in more complexities.
  - Include leads or lag time.
  - Draw dependency diagrams:
    - **Activity on Node** (AON) or precedence diagram (the most common style for depicting activity dependencies). Suggested by Project Management Institute (PMI) group.

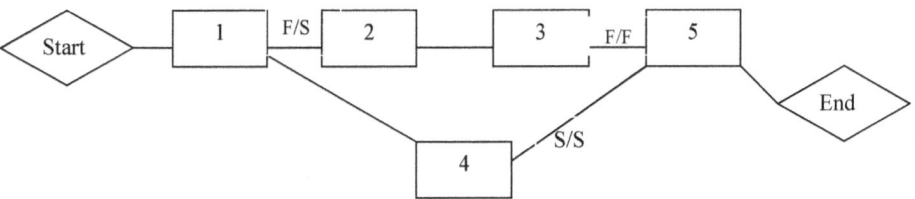

Here are the characteristics of this diagram:
- Task 1 has tasks 2 and 4 as its successors
- Task 2 has task 3 as its successor
- Task 5 has tasks 4 and 3 as its predecessor.
- Start/start relationship between 4 and 5.
- Finish/finish relationship between 3 and 5.
- F/S between relationship between 1 and 2.
- Tasks are put on the node/box.

    - **Activity on Arrow (AOA)**—This type of dependency diagram is rarely used on projects. The activities are represented by the arrows connecting the nodes. The nodes are typically circles as shown in the following diagram:

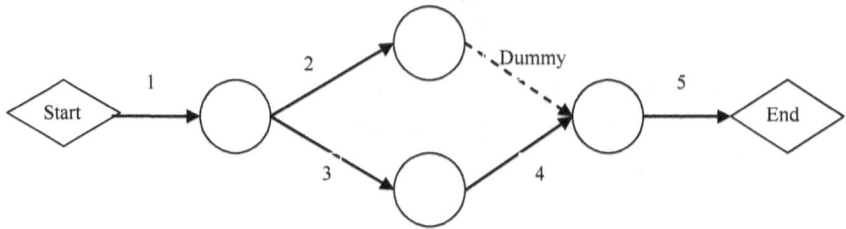

Here are the characteristics of this diagram:

- The activities are on the arrows.
- There is no information in the nodes, but they are there to allow us to create dependencies.
- Tasks 2 and 3 are dependent on 1.
- Task 4 is dependent on 3.
- A dummy node is created to allow task 2 to depend on the end of the project and task 5.
- The dotted arrow indicates a dummy activity.
- It only represents finish/start style relationship.

- **Estimate Activity Resources**
  - Use the project scope, project blueprint, and work breakdown structure to determine the following:
    - The needed resources from goods, supplies, and people standpoints.
    - The quantities of resources needed on the project.
    - When are the resources needed?
- **Estimate Activity Durations**
  - The estimation of activity duration is needed to develop an accurate schedule. The input for estimating duration includes the following:
    - Resource Calendar
      - The following factors must be considered when scheduling resource availability. For example,
        - forty hours does not equal forty hours,
        - full-time resource for forty-hour workweek,
        - sick time,

- o read e-mail,
- o vacation time, and
- o attending department meetings.
  - Estimated Activity Resources
  - Project Scope Baseline
  - Organization Process Assets or and Project Historical Information
- o Methods for estimating duration accurately include
  - **g**uess/roll dice,
  - Monte Carlo analysis,
  - analogous estimation,
  - *p*arameter driven,
  - *b*ottom-up estimating,
  - *m*ultiple estimators (compare savings), and
  - PERT (Program Evaluation Review Technique). Developing multiple estimates for each tasks:
    - Pessimistic (P), Optimistic (O), and a Most Likely (ML)
    - (P + 4ML + O) divide by 6 = Estimate
- o In general, the following factor must be considered when estimating duration:
  - Amount of work.
  - Team.
  - Actual effort, not duration.
  - Forty hours work.
  - One resource = one week.
  - Focused on the amount of work required to complete the job, not the duration.
  - Software applications may be used to calculate the duration leaving time to focus on work required to complete the tasks.

- **Develop Schedule**
  - o Using a software preferably, although this may be done manually, develop the project schedule using the following inputs:
    - Work Breakdown Structure (WBS)
    - Dependencies among tasks
    - Duration estimates
  - o Iterate through the process to develop the final schedule.
- **Control Schedule**
  - o This process involves having a number of methods in place to track progress, integrate changes, and manage against project

schedule baseline. The specific methods and details are as follows:

- **Critical Path Method**

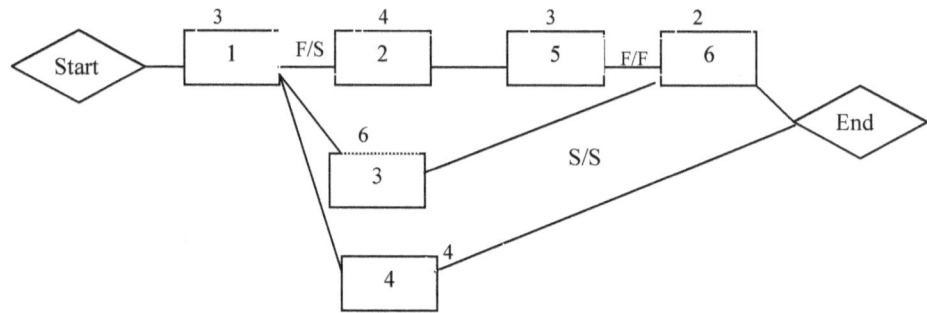

- ▪ The critical path is the path in the plan that has the longest duration to the end of the project. This effectively determines the end date of the project.
- ▪ The critical path in the above diagram is route tasks 1, 2, 5, and 6 (duration: 3, 4, 3, 3) = 12.
- ▪ Control and monitor the tasks on the critical path to make sure nothing impacts them because they affect the end of the project.
- ▪ Monitor tasks that are near the critical path that may become critical path due to small changes.
- ▪ This is the most effective method for monitoring the end date of a project.
- ▪ A project management tool may be used to calculate for near critical path, that is, the *slack* or *float*. The bigger the slack (or float), the further away from critical path.

- **Resource Leveling**
  - ▪ This is the development of a project schedule based on limited resources. A resource-limited schedule is developed
    - • to ensure an optimal team size for the project and
    - • to ensure full utilization of resources.
  - ▪ A coco model may be used to determine the optimal team size.

The following resource level chart that shows the utilization distribution on a project:

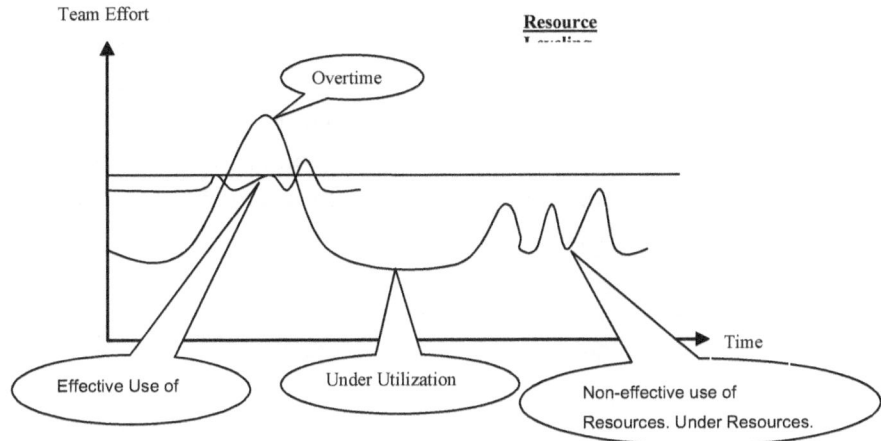

- ○ **Track Progress**
  - ▪ Team must provide weekly status report, inclusive of report time needed and remaining to complete a task.
  - ▪ Work with team members to get information on tracking project schedule.
  - ▪ This could be a tasking process, but work with the team to track progress.
- ○ **Integrate Changes**
  - ▪ Integrate changes into the project schedule.
  - ▪ The project software will recalculate the project plan. It is necessary to work with team members to ensure project timeline is not drastically affected in the project.
  - ▪ Implement effective change management process. Update project plan based on approved changes.
  - ▪ Manage against baseline. Measure changes against baseline and manage accordingly.
- ○ **Schedule Compression**
  - ▪ There are two commonly used methods for schedule compression:

- **Fast Tracking**
  - What can be done to make the project progress faster?
  - Review dependencies and eliminate where possible. Make the tasks run in parallel where possible.
  - Introduce lag where possible and start some tasks earlier.
  - Cost may not be increased, but project risk is slightly increased since original dependencies as discretionary are ignored, and parallel execution of tasks has now been introduced.
- **Crashing**
  - Change project environment to improve end date.
  - Introduce new resources, but aim for the optimal number of resources.
  - Introduce new project management tools to facilitate the process.
  - Cost is certainly increased. Too many resources do not necessarily improve project schedule linearly.
  - Examine critical path tasks for schedule compression since they have the highest impact on the project end date.

Chapter 13: Cost Management

Project cost management is for managing the processes to ensure that projects are completed within the approved budget. These processes include estimating, budgeting, and controlling costs. The following sections describe the processes of project cost management:

- **Estimate Cost**
  - Create detailed estimate for each and every elements in the work breakdown structure. The total project cost estimate must include the following:
    - Cost to deliver each work breakdown structure element.
    - Cost of human resources.
    - Cost of materials.
    - Cost of Supplies.
    - Project life cycle costing (trade-off analysis). Spend more now on planning and design and spend less later on implementation, verification, and maintenance.
    - Cost of quality.
    - Cost of overheads.
  - The cost to be estimated may be classified into the following:
    - **Direct Costs**—Direct salary cost of team, direct cost for purchasing material.
    - **Indirect Costs**—Fringe benefits, insurance, telephone charges, supporting cost for the projects. Storage, transportation, hotel bills, etc.
    - **Fixed Costs**—Cost a unit for a resource, material, and equipment.
    - **Variable Costs**—For every unit, hour, supply, or time, there is a cost associated with the usage.

- **Sunk Cost**—Unrecoverable cost that have been expended upon a project.
- Cost Variance
  - The change of cost over time must be considered when estimating cost. For example, inflation and depreciation of materials (e.g., vehicles, computers).
  - The change of cost over volume. Supplier's agreement (one to ten quantity cost more than eleven to one hundred in quantity).
- Estimating Technique
  - Techniques for estimating cost for order of magnitude, conceptual, preliminary, definitive to control estimates include the following:
    - Analogous Estimation—Expert judgment based on history and previous experience.
    - Parametric Estimation—Parametric unit cost times the number of required units.
    - Unit Cost Based on Effort—Cost of resources.
    - Vendor Bids/Fixed Price Analysis—What is the cost of project per vendor?
    - Bottom-Up Estimating—The most accurate method. The cost estimation at work packages or activities level.
    - Three-Point Estimates—PERT (Program Evaluation Review Technique).
- Estimation Type
  - The following are some of the type of estimation that could be used for cost estimation and also applicable to time estimation:
    - Rough Order of Magnitude [-50% to +100%]
    - Conceptual Estimate [-30% to +50%]
    - Preliminary Estimate [-20% to 30%]
    - Budget Estimate [-5% to +10%]
    - Definitive Estimate [-15% to +20%]
    - Control Estimate [-10% to 15%]
- **Determine Budget**
  - This is the summation of individual cost estimates to determine the total project cost or cost performance baseline. This process also involves dealing with cash management and forecasting. The cost budget should include the following:

- Aggregated Costs—The cost aggregation of direct, indirect, fixed, and variable costs.
- Developed cash flow that is based on the estimates—A month-per-month cash flow for cash management.
- Cost Baseline—Approved changes in estimated total project cost.
- Contingency (unknown cost variance). The need to have reserve for contingency.

o A practical approach to determining cost budget (using a bottom approach on the work breakdown structure) is cost aggregation.
- Work Package Cost = Cost of Activities
- Control Account = Sum of Work Package Costs
- Project Cost = Sum of Control Accounts in the Project
- Cost Performance Baseline = Contingency Reserve + Project Cost
- Cost Budget = Management Reserve + Cost Performance Baseline

o The accuracy of the determined budget for effective cost management and control is aided by applying the following in the summation process:
  i. Round the budget to the next appropriate level (to the thousandths, hundredths, etc.).
  ii. Define project budget with degree of precision +/-50%.
  iii. Define project budget with degree of confidence.

o Project Budget Accounting—Every organization has a defined approach for defining their budget within an accounting principle. The project manager is expected to work with their account department on how budgeting is done. The following accounting principles that is common to most organizations may be use to qualify project viability (or selection) for budgeting and implementation:
- **Present Value (PV)**—Apply an expectation of future interest rate to determine the current value of money to be spent on a project (or future value, apply future interest rate to determine the return on the money to be spent). It might be better to keep the money in the bank for better return at the end of the term. Higher present value is desirable.
- **Net Present Value (NPV)**—This is the same as the present value but with the cost of project factored into the calculation.

- **Rate of Return (ROR)**—The expected rate of return, inflation, and interest rate.
- **Payback Period**—What is the length of return? Shorter payback period is preferred.
- **Return on Investment (ROI)**—The bigger, the better is the project for investment.
- **Return on Investment Capital (ROIC)**—The higher, the better. Net income divided by capital invested.
- **Internal Rate of Return (IRR)**—If the project was an interest rate, what would you prefer? Bigger is better.
- **Benefit Cost Ratio (BCR)**—Greater than one is good.
- **Economic Value Add (EVA)**—After tax profit.
- **Opportunity Cost**—The smaller the opportunity cost of choosing a project, the better the project. This is really the cost of the other opportunities missed.
- **Control Costs**
  - This is a proactive process to ensure that spending on a project is monitored and controlled. It ensures that costs in a project are within the planned budget and any change in costs is easily detected.
  - The proactive approach for controlling costs include the following:
    - *Manage cost baseline per month.* The goal of this process is to deliver on budget and to the plan cash flow. It ensures that the project expenditure is in line with the plan, and project needs are in line with the planned cash flow.
    - *Manage variances.* Measure the variances, manage and adjust the cost baseline if necessary. Adjustment to the cost baseline will need the approval of senior management and project sponsor.
    - *Manage budget performance.* Monitor how project is progressing—on time, on budget; on time, below budget, etc.

Expanded View of Cost Control

Cost management is about cost estimating and ensuring that project is delivered within budget with measures and control in place. The following is an expanded view of the measures to have in place for monitoring the cost of a project.

Manage Baseline

1. Review and approve charges on the project.
2. Manage changes.
   a. *Approved changes.* Manage changes through the change control process to ensure integrated change control of project baseline.
   b. *Estimate variances.* Manage time spent on project activities to minimize variances on cost. The pluses and minuses of the variances should be managed and communicated to the appropriate management. Make adjustment where necessary to keep project within budget.
   c. *Price variances.* Monitor price estimates and actual prices of materials and resources. Manage all price variances to ensure all variances are within the project budget.
   d. You may reduce scope based on approved changes to adjust baseline cost.
3. Monitor the coding of charges.
4. Charges are mapped to the appropriate project code.
5. Monitor invoices and the mapping of project codes.
6. Monitor vendor payment and all charges applied to the project.

Manage Variances

1. Variances in project management plan are inevitable. Gather the facts that are causing variances on the project and address those facts.
2. *Variance analysis.* Do the root-cause analysis to see what can be done to improve the variances.
3. *Trend analysis.* Measure the trends of changes in amount versus time. Plot the actual cost against cost baseline for detailed analysis of trends on the project. The following graph is a representation of managing variances with trend analysis.

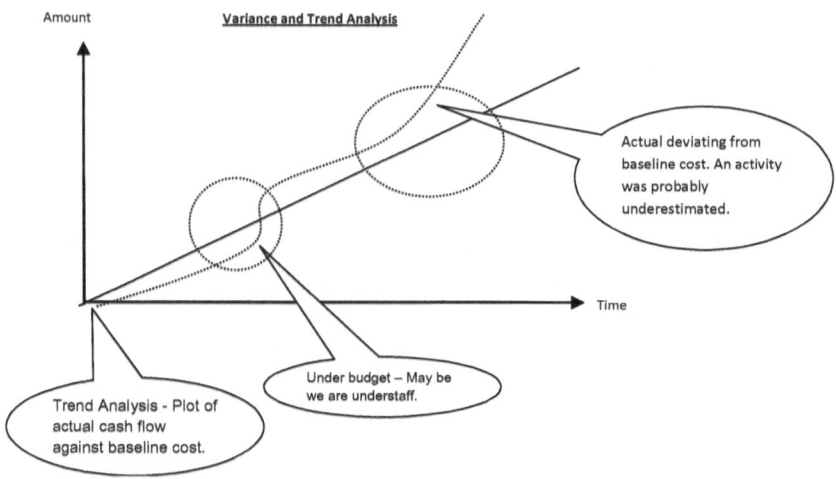

Manage Budget Performance

The management of budget performance is done using various performance measurement techniques including the following:

- **Earned value analysis**—The measuring of actual project performance against original plan. The earned value technique involves mapping budget to schedule and developing the key values for the measurement of scheduled activity, work packages, or control accounts. The following *formulas* define the key performance indicators when earned value analysis is being used to manage budget performance:
  - Planned Value (PV) = The percentage of work that should have been completed at a point in time × Budget at Completion (BAC).
  - Earned Value (EV) = Percentage of work actually completed × Budget at Completion (BAC).
  - Actual Cost (AC)—This is the actual cost of the project.
  - Cost Variance (CV) = Earned Value (EV)—Actual Cost (AC).
  - Schedule Variance (SV) = Earned Value (EV)—Planned Value (PV).
  - Cost Performance Index (CPI) = Earned Value (EV) / Actual Cost (AC).
  - Schedule Performance Index (SPI) = Earned Value (EV) / Planned Value (PV).

- **Forecasting**—The estimation of project cost based on project work performance and any supporting information that could impact the project. The key performance indicators that could help to assess the cost or amount of work to complete the schedule activities include the following:
  - Estimate at Completion (EAC) = Budget at Completion (BAC) / Cost Performance Completion
  - Estimate to Completion (ETC) = Estimate at Completion (EAC)—Actual Cost (AC)
  - Variance at Completion (VAC) = Budget at Completion (BAC)—Estimate at Completion (EAC).
  - To-Complete Performance Index (TCPIc) = (BAC-EV) / Remaining Funds.
- **Project Performance Review**—A schedule-based performance review to measure budget and deliverable of milestones. The indicators of performance review include the following:
  - On Time-On Budget—The project is on time and to budget.
  - Ahead-Overbudget—The project is ahead of time and overbudget.
  - Ahead-Underbudget—The project is ahead of time and underbudget.
  - Behind-Overbudget—The project is behind schedule and it is overbudget. This is a bad state of project.
  - Behind-Under budget—The project is behind schedule and it is under budget. Adjustment must be made to the schedule or budget for project to continue successfully.

Chapter 14: Quality Management

What is Quality?

- Quality is delivering product that is in conformance to requirements, delivering product or services that is fit to use, satisfying the customer (no gold plating—delivering more than promised—because quality will be compromised), building prevention into the project quality plan rather than inspection, continuous process improvement, and building quality process and standards into the project plan.

The following project quality management processes determine the policies, objectives, and responsibilities expected from a project to meet the requirements from the customer or sponsor. Project quality management consists of the following:

- **Plan Quality**—This is to identify the quality expectations to be built into the project and to ensure that the quality process is well defined and communicated in the project. The following steps are followed when defining the quality plan:
  - Define Quality Management Plan
    - Build quality into the plan. The project quality management plan should include team inspections, walkthrough, and review. Build the time into the project plan.
  - Define quality metrics and standards based on the type of project.
  - Define quality checklist.
  - Build in customer quality expectations. What is acceptable by the customer or project sponsor?
  - What is the acceptable tolerance of error?

- ○ **Perform Quality Assurance**—This is to ensure that quality plan is followed through in the project. To ensure a quality plan, follow a change request approach (perform integrated change control). do the *right* things. Ensure that review take place and the right resources take part in the review process. *d*o things better. Review the quality assurance process. Are we doing it right? *c*ontinuous process improvement—the root cause analysis. Why are there errors in the project? audit. Use quality metrics for measurement.

- • **Perform Quality Control**—This is to ensure that we are doing the right thing and delivering the right results. To perform quality control, follow these steps:
  - ○ Perform quality control measurement.
  - ○ Validate changes.
  - ○ Validate deliverables.
  - ○ The resulting product is fit to use. Business requirements are met by the results.
  - ○ Deliverable is inspected, measured, and tested.
    - ▪ Process of quality control includes inspection, testing, sampling, and statistical control.

Other Related Quality Standards

- ○ **Total Quality Management (TQM)—A quality management process that r**equires all individual in the company to be responsible for quality, shifts quality from product to process of producing products, and focuses on improvement in process and results.
- • **International Standard Organization (ISO)**—a voluntary, nontreaty federation of standards setting bodies of some 130 countries. Founded in 1946-47 in Geneva as a UN agency, it promotes development of standardization and related activities to facilitate international trade in goods and services and cooperation on economic, intellectual, scientific, and technological aspects. (Source: *www.businessdictionary.com*) ISO 9000—A standard for performing quality assurance.
- • **Six Sigma**—Six Sigma seeks to improve the quality of process outputs by identifying and removing the causes of defects (errors)

and minimizing variability in manufacturing and business processes. It uses a set of quality management methods, including statistical methods, and creates a special infrastructure of people within the organization ("Black Belts," "Green Belts," etc.) who are experts in these methods. (Source: http://en.wikipedia.org)

- **Juran Crosby Deming**—
  - **Crosby**—It is conformance to requirements, not as goodness. It is management's job to set the requirements and communicate to employees.
  - **Deming**—Meeting and exceeding the customer's need and expectations and then continuing to improve.
  - **Juran**—Quality mission of the company is "fitness for use" as perceived by customers. The missions of individual departments are to work according to specifications designed to achieve fitness for use.
- **KAIZEN (Continuous Improvement)**—Japanese management term.
  - Constant process improvement.
- **Just-in-Time (JIT)**—A production strategy that strives to improve a business' return on investment by reducing in-process inventory and associated carrying costs.
  - Zero or near zero inventory
  - Focuses on quality
  - No excess inventory

Why prevention should be emphasized in quality plan

- Prevention is keeping defects from occurring in the project.
- Inspection is catching errors that have occurred in the results of the project.
- It is cheaper to fix issues at prevention level.
- Fixes are costly at inspection level.
- See graph below:

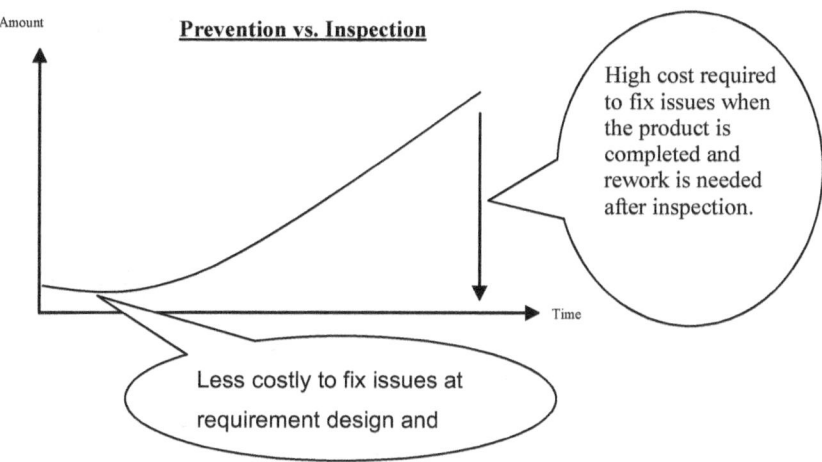

Methods of Quality Control

- **Cause and Effect Diagram (Ishikawa Diagram or Fishbone Diagram)**—This is a method of determine the effect of various factors on a potential problem. The diagram provides visibility to potential cause of a problem:

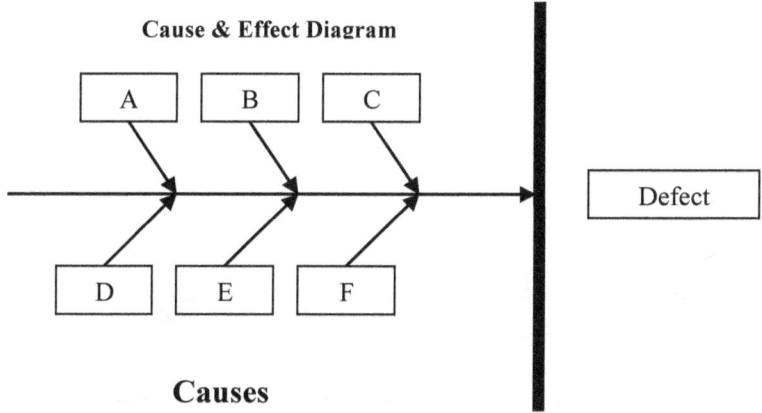

- **Pareto Chart**—This is the application of the 80/20 rule. Generally used to identify and evaluate nonconformities. The 80% of the problems are due to 20% of the causes. Fix the 20% of the problems that are major hits due to time constraints because the majority of the problems are within the 20%. The 80% of our time is spent fixing A, B, C (20%).

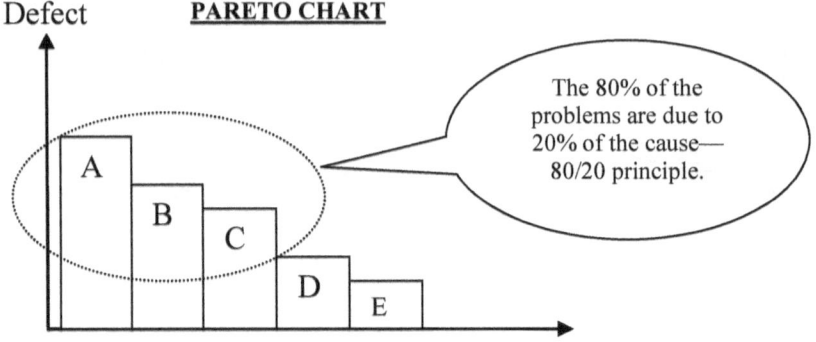

- **Control Charts**—Control charts are for monitoring project and product life cycle process. Control charts are for determining the stability and predictable performance on a project or product life cycle process. The steps for using control charts include the following:
  - ○ Establish the midpoint for measuring the success of the project.
  - ○ Plot measurements to make sure projects are within the limits of quality.
  - ○ Take corrective actions to bring project back to midpoint.
  - ○ Use the rule of 7 where necessary.

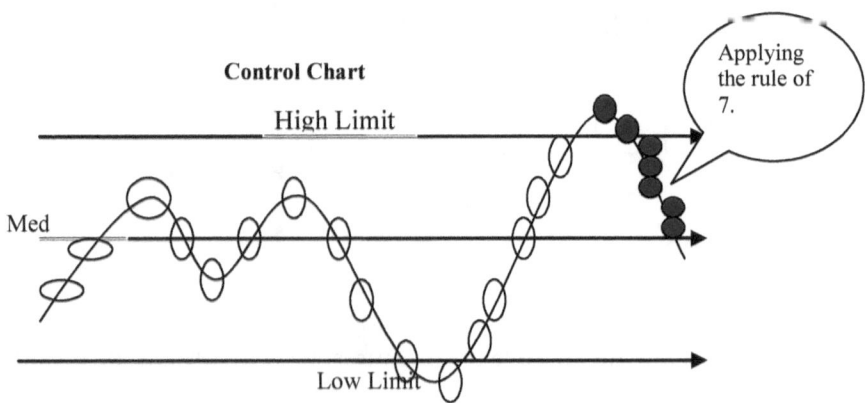

- **Standard Deviation (Six Sigma)**—Standard deviation is used to set quality levels and control limits.

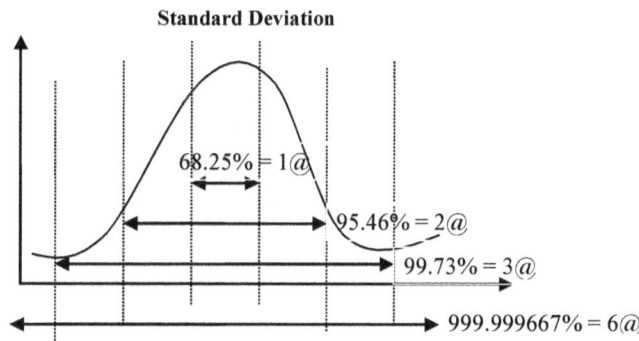

- o The following defines the steps of Six Sigma:
  - It uses bell curve.
  - Most organizations aim for Six Sigma.
  - Use Six Sigma to refine the quality process.
  - Use the appropriate sigma level base on time and money.

- **Tolerance versus Control Limits**—Tolerance is the acceptable limit set for product quality. Control limits are acceptable variances in project or product life cycle process. The following diagram shows a process operating within a 3-sigma control limits.

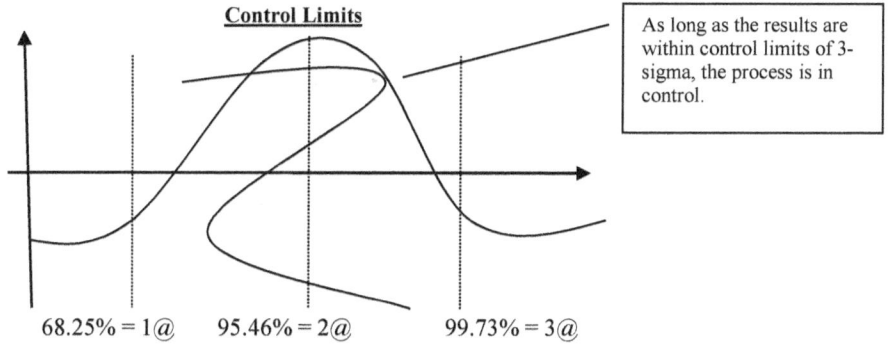

- Other quality control tools include as follows:
  - **Benchmarking**—The measurement of project results against previous projects.
  - **Run Charts**—It shows the history and pattern of variations.
  - **Scatter Diagrams**—It shows the pattern of relationship between control variables.
  - **Sampling**
    - Statistical Sampling—Random sampling of products to minimize overall quality control measurement costs.
    - Variable Sampling—Measuring closeness to quality conformance.
    - Attribute Sampling—Product either conforms to quality or it does not. Discreet measurement method—one or zero, 100% or 0.
  - **Inspection**—The examination of product for quality conformance.
  - **Defect Review**—This could be peer review or management review of deliverable defects.

Per PMI standards, project quality management expects project manager to deliver what has been promised and only what has been promised in the project scope. There should be no gold plating. Do not deliver more than what has been promised because quality will be compromised.

Chapter 15: Human Resource Management

Human resource management process requires soft skills and the need for the project manager to develop a style of dealing with project team or human resources. A method personalized for dealing with team motivation, conflict resolution, support, and interacting with team members. It may be necessary for the project manager to deliver a style of project management consistent to his or her personality. The following are the processes in human resources management:

- **Develop human resource plan.** Develop a plan that details the human resources requirement for the project. The plan should include the level of skills required for the areas of work in the project. The human resource plan is a section of the project management plan. The following should be considered when developing the human resources plan:
  - Define the needed skills.
  - Define when the resources are needed on the project.
  - Define the number of skilled analyst required.
  - Define how long the resources are needed on the project.
  - Provide a transition plan if necessary.
  - Provide a staff rotation plan if necessary.
  - Define the level of authority required in the project.
- **Develop Project Org Chart**. Draw the organization chart to show reporting structure. Draw both the project and the organization charts to understand the possible conflicts, career aspirations, relationships between management structures:

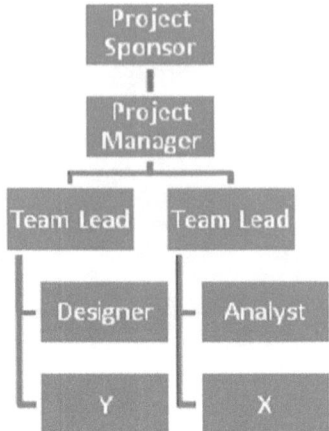

- **Define Roles and Responsibilities**. Define the roles and responsibilities for the following resources, decision makers, escalation levels, etc.:
  - Project manager.
  - Stakeholders.
  - Senior management. They will be accepting the final deliverables, etc.
  - Sponsor/acceptor.
  - Functional manager.
  - Team for status reporting.
  - RACI matrix is a chart for the illustration of the roles and responsibilities on a project. RACI stands for **R**esponsible **A**ccountable **C**onsult **I**nform. This may also be referred to as RAM, **R**esponsibility **A**ssignment **M**atrix.

- **Acquire Project Team.** This is the staffing of project with the type of resources described in the project management plan. If experiencing challenges in staffing project due to lack of required resource, make changes in the human resources plan to accommodate the challenges.
  - Develop staff assignment.
  - Develop resource calendar.

- **Develop Project Team**. The project manager has the responsibility to develop the project team for project to be delivered on time, on budget to project scope. The following should be provided to the project team:

o   Training.
o   Ground rules—Formal and informal rules that defines the boundaries on the project.
o   Team building activities.
o   Interpersonal skills (soft skills).
o   Co-location or war room on project site.
o   Motivation using recognition and reward theories—These theories include the following:

  ▪ **Maslow Hierarchy of Needs**—The lower needs must be satisfied before people can reach their upper needs using the following hierarchy from Abraham Maslow:

  ▪ **McGregor's Theory X and Y Theory**
    • Theory X—People are lazy by default. They need constant supervision to achieve desire result.
    • Theory Y—People are motivated naturally to do good work.

  ▪ **Herzberg**—The presence of certain factor does not make staff satisfied. But lack of it will dissatisfy the staff.

  ▪ **Contingency Theory**
    • The effectiveness of a leader is dependent on whether the leader is task oriented or relationship oriented.

- Situational Factors—Task oriented is more suitable for stressful environment. But a balance in human relationship may also be needed for the success of the project.

  - **McClelland's Three-Need Theory**—The achievement theory.
    - The desire for achievement. High achievers group together.
    - The desire for power. Social or individual power.
    - The desire for affiliation (with a team).

  - **Forms of Project Manager Power**
    - Formal or Legitimate—Due by position.
    - Reward—Motivate with a reward.
    - Punishment—A coercive power if goal is not met by team member.
    - Expert—Power of knowledge on a subject.
    - Referent—Power of respect and personality.

- **Manage Project Team**—The project manager has the responsibility to coordinate project team, track team member, and project performance, manage project changes, and resolve any conflicts. Specific methods to be used by project manager are as follows:
  - **Observation and Conversation**—Manage day-to-day project activities by working with team members on status update, monitoring progress, and communicating on any pending issues.
  - **Project Performance Appraisal**—Appraise individuals on their job performance on the project.
  - **Manage Conflicts**—Encourage positive project working environment by resolving conflicts as they surface on the project. The following are known methods for resolving conflicts and roles recognition that facilitates the ability to resolve the conflicts:
    - **Conflict Resolution Methods**
      - **Problem Solving (Confrontation)**—Recommended by PMI group to be the best approach because it involves addressing the conflict head-on to a resolution. Address the issue, *not* the person.

- **Compromise**—A lose-lose approach to resolve the conflict. A deadlock situation resolution.
- **Forcing**—The use of force to resolve conflict is generally least accepted. It may reduce morale on the project, and damaging in the long term.
- **Smoothing**—This is an attempt to diminish the problem. It is not really solved but may be appropriate for certain situation.
- **Withdrawal**—This is an avoidance approach with the hope that the problem will go away.

- **Role Types**
  - **Constructive Roles**
    - Initiator—Thinker
    - Encourager—Motivator
    - Information seeker
    - Information giver
    - Clarifiers
    - Harmonizers
    - Summarizers
    - Gatekeepers
    - Director
    - **Destructive Roles**
    - Aggressors
    - Blockers
    - Withdrawers
    - Recognition seekers
    - Topic jumpers
    - Dominator
    - Devil's advocate

The project manager must determine his or her personality to balance hard and soft skills to effectively manage a project. Experience has shown that individuals are generally not in favor of being managed because change in behavior is required. Project managers should to focus on managing the project work and not the people, while maintaining a work-life balance for the resources on the project, if that make sense.

Chapter 16: Communication Management

Project communication management is the coordination of processes that identifies stakeholders and ensures timely, appropriate, and effective communication of project information to the stakeholders. The processes in project communication management include the following:

- **Identify stakeholders.** This is an initiating process. It involves identifying all the respective stakeholders that will be affected positively or negatively by the implementation of this project.
- **Plan communication.** A planning process. It involves planning and determining what project information and how it will be communicated to the respective project stakeholders. Complete the communication management plan that feeds into the project management plan. The communication management plan consist of
  - the frequency of communication distribution and
  - the format of communication or communication techniques.
    - **Style of Communication**
      - Interactive—Two—or multiple-way communication.
      - Pull—Requesting for status or feedback.
      - Push—Announcing or presenting information.
    - **Methods of Communication**
      - **Informal Written**
  - Memos and e-mails—Type professional-looking e-mail that delivers the right message.
      - **Formal Written**
  - Reports
  - Contracts
  - Legal document
  - Project document

- ○ Project Websites—Develop simple project websites to help organize project
  - **Informal Verbal**
- ○ In person
- ○ Instant messengers
- ○ Phone calls
- ○ Meetings
- ○ Discussions
  - **Formal Verbal**
- ○ Presentations—good quality presentation, professional
- ○ Conference calls
- ○ Speeches
- ○ Mass communication
- ○ What information to distribute:
  - Status—The good and bad news of the project status.
  - Plan Updates—Change management. Implementing changes to the project.
  - Team Performance—Time spent on tasks from team members. Status report from team members.
  - Meetings—A well-managed meeting can be very effective for project communication.
  - Problems—The project communication must be open to problem communication from stakeholders, team members, and project manager.
- ○ Which stakeholder will receive information:
  - Stakeholder Register—List of identified risks.
- ○ **Distribute Information**—An executing process to communicate the planned project information. The objective of this process is to ensure that the right information is distributed to the right people (or project stakeholder) at the right time, in the right format, in the right place; to ensure that the requirements of the project are delivered as expected; and to distribute project performance report.
- • **Manage Stakeholders Expectations**—A monitor and control process to communicate with stakeholders and to ensure that they are in tune with project update and expectations.
  - ○ *Communicate.* Make sure stakeholders are getting what they expect and what has been promised to them.

- ○ *Follow up on issues*. Create an issue log for all promises to the stakeholders. Track all promises and issues in the issue log.
- **Report Performance**—A monitor and control process to gather details on project requirements or expectations and report on what has been delivered for performance measurement. The following are some of the information to be reported:
  - ○ Project weekly status.
  - ○ Project monthly status.
  - ○ Progress and milestones—consolidated team status report.
  - ○ Stakeholder management.
  - ○ Consistency—Be consistent in the status report delivery, issues and meetings status reporting.

Communication Channel

As part of analyzing communication requirement and determining which stakeholder should receive project communication, it is required that the communication channel and the path of communication should be determined:

$$\text{Communication Channels} = [n \times (n-1)]/2$$

Communication Model

Further analysis into the communication requirement is the communication model. Messages are conveyed in sender-receiver model, and to ensure that they are conveyed correctly, it is necessary to study the receiver's response to the sent messages. The following are the models of communication commonly used:

- **Active Listening**—The receiver of message constantly indicate successful reception and comprehension of message.
- **Effective Listening**—Similar to active listening. Indicate with vocal or body language the understanding of message received with full attention to sender's message.

- **Feedback**—Receiver constantly provides feedback on message received, whether it is understood or unclear.
- **Nonverbal**—Constant indication with body language on the clarity of message received.
- **Paralingual**—These are vocal signs to indicate receiver's attention to messages being received from sender. Pitch and tone of voice are used for this process.

Chapter 17: Risk Management

Project risk management is the management of processes that identify and analyze risks, plans risk responses, monitors and controls factors contributing to risks on a project. It involves dealing with the unknowns; it can be very challenging and difficult. Project risk management consists of the following processes:

- **Plan Risk Management**—Developing the strategy for dealing with risk or managing risk. Creating an overall plan for risk management. The risk management plan should include the following:
  - **Executive Summary**—An overall strategy for managing risk on the project. A detailed analysis of stakeholders' openness to risks will help in defining the executive summary.
    - Are *stakeholders* (including project sponsor) risk seekers or avoiders? High-profile projects are generally risk avoiders because of the project cost.
    - *Corporate factors*—Is this a risk-taking corporate environment or risk-avoidance organization. There may be resistance if the strategy does not go along with the corporate strategy.
  - **Risk Management Approach**—The process or approach to be followed in identifying risk on the project and managing the risks. How rigorous is risk management on the project?
    - **History/Experience**—Based organization or project history, build into the plan the risk profile. This should help to define the approach for managing risk on the project.
  - **Roles and Responsibilities of Stakeholders**—Define the roles and responsibilities of stakeholders in managing risks. Who is responsible for risk management on the project?

- ○ **Categorization of Risk**—Rate risk on scale of low, medium, or high based on probabilities and impact assessments. High risks are dealt with followed by medium risks, then low-rated risks.
- ○ **Budgeting**—Budget for the risk measures in the project cost baseline.
- ○ **Risk Probabilities and Impact**—This is the qualitative analysis of risk to measure the different levels of risk probabilities and impact on the project. The result of this assessment is included in the risk management plan for project references.

- • **Identify Risks**—Risks are components to the events that involve uncertainties or unplanned activities. Risks may affect a project positively. Reducing cost and time of a project or negatively increasing cost and time. Risk identification is an iterative process that deals with how unknown risks or uncertainties are identified and documented as risk register. The project management plan, scope, and other environmental factors are considered when identifying the risks on a project.
  - ○ **Factors to be considered when identifying risks**:
    - ▪ **Known Risk**—For example, training is needed for the deployment of a new system. There may be some issues after deployment because training is required. Time and money may be required for training.
    - ▪ **Unknown Risks**—Allocate additional time and money for unknown risks. Contingency is required. Create funding for the known and unknown risks (contingency funds).
    - ▪ **Source of Risk**—The following are possible source of risk on the project:
      - • Technology Risk—Known and unknown technology issues, money, and time allocation.
      - • Team—How corporative is the team? More risks with less corporative team.
      - • Scope—Loosely defined scope means more risk.
      - • Business—How stable is the business?
      - • Economy—Good or bad economy?
      - • Competition—Is company leading competition a possible higher risk?

- **Risk Identification Techniques**—What techniques are available to this project?
  - **Brainstorming**—Set up a team or brainstorming session to identify all possible or probable risks on the project.
  - **Delphi Technique**—Use project experts on the project to identify risks based on their experience.
  - **Interviews**—Interview individuals, businesses, and stakeholders on project to identify the risk factors that can affect the success of the project.
  - **Root Cause Analysis**—Apply root cause analysis or the Ishikawa diagram to drill down in detail into project risks.
  - **SWOT Analysis**—Strength, Weakness, Opportunities, and Threats analysis of project based on experience.

- **Qualitative Risk**—This is the ranking and prioritization of risks based on their level of probability of impacting the project. The project organization can focus on high-priority risks that will impact timeline while lower priority risks are addressed as time and cost permit on the project. To facilitate qualitative risk analysis is the probability and impact matrix used for risk assessment based on cost, time, scope, and quality. The following is a format for the probability and impact matrix:

Project Objective	Low(1)	Medium(3)	High(7)	Very High(9)
Cost	Insignificant	<5%	<10%	>10%
Time	Insignificant	<10 days	<25days	>25days
Scope	Insignificant	No business Impact	Some business problems	Definite business impact
Quality	Insignificant	No anticipated problems	Potential Line Problems	Definite Problems
Result	Low			
Ranking	Cost < 5% (Medium) Time > 27days (High)			

- **Quantitative Analysis**—This process focuses on project risks that require the most attention because of their impact on the project timeline. The purpose of quantitative risk analysis include the following:
  - Analysis of high-impact risks—These are risks that require high money value.
  - Numeric rating of risks—Quantify risk in money value.
  - Risk impact simulation—A technique such as Monte Carlo simulation software may be used for this analysis and calculation.
  - Decision Tree—A decision tree may be drawn as shown to determine shower down impact. The following example shows the cost impact of price increase on the equipment required to deploy a project, and the cost impact of not providing training on the new system to be deployed.

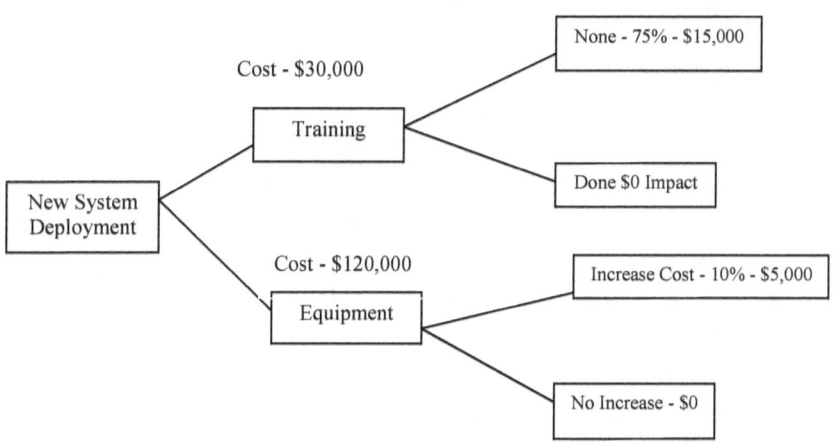

  - The following table is the numerical analysis of the decision tree:

	Initial Cost	Risk Cost	Probability	Total
Training	$30,000.00	$15,000.00	75%	$30,000.00 + ($15,000.00 x 75%) = $41,250.00
Equipment	$120,000.00	$5,000.00	10%	$120,000.00 + ($5000 x 10%) = $120,500.00

  - Training requires a minimum contingency amount of $41,250.00.
  - Equipment requires a minimum contingency amount of $120,500.00.

- **Plan Risk Response**—This is the process of planning how all the analyzed risk in the risk registered will be managed or handled. Planning ahead of time on how threats will be eliminated or probabilities of threats will be decreased and increasing the probabilities of opportunities on the project. The plan should include clearly defined strategies for threats and opportunities.
  - **Strategies for threats are as follows**:
    - *Avoid.* Change the plan by removing the threat.
    - *Transfer.* Insurance—Transfer risk to a third party or contract out project to qualified contractor or external firm.
    - *Mitigate.* What can you do to lessen the impact? Risk cannot be eliminated but can be lessen or mitigated. Provide training to minimize risk but provide contingency plan to cover risk just in case.
    - *Accept.* There are some project risks that you might have to just accept. Put a contingency amount and/or time to accept contingency risk.
  - **Strategies for opportunities include the following**:
    - *Exploit.* Change project management plan to ensure opportunity occur. For example, project may be completed earlier before the plan date. Add more resources to exploit opportunity.
    - *Share.* Government project might require partnering with small businesses to win government contracts. Partner with small businesses to achieve the positive risk or opportunity of winning large government contracts.
    - *Enhance.* Do not mitigate risk here but increase the probability of the risk or opportunity.
    - *Accept.* This also applies to opportunities. Sudden discovery of training requirement for unplanned system or business activity. Training can be a source of revenue for the organization.

- **Monitor and Control of Risk**—The purposes of this process are as follows:
  - **Monitor known risks**
    - **Risk Register**—Track the status of risks listed in the risk register. Monitor the risks per timeline and deal with the risks

that are near timeline. The following is a sample risk register table:

Risk Register				
Risk Item	Probability Impact	Risk Management Strategy	Critical Dates	Current Status
Inadequate Training	Medium	Mitigate	This Week	No Issues
Increase Equipment Prices	High	Accept	This month	Review Periodically

- **Monitor Risk Profile**—Monitor risks based on the information in the risk profile to mitigate the impact of the risks. High-profile risks are of high urgency, or high-impact risk should receive more focus.
  - o **Assess Risks**—Look out for new risk in the following:
    - Scope changes—Monitor scope changes and impact on schedule and cost.
    - Schedule changes—Monitor schedule changes due to new risks.
    - Environment changes—Monitor impact of environmental changes.
    - Interview project stakeholders.
  - o **Manage Contingency**—Ensure fund allocated for contingency are spent only on the risk.
  - o **Audit Risks**—Audit the overall risk management process to ensure that risk is properly managed on the project.
  - o **Status Meetings**—Hold frequent status meetings to discuss status.

Chapter 18: Procurement Management

Procurement management is management of processes to acquire and purchase goods and services required for the project. A contract may be applied depending on the scale of the purchase. This is to ensure that the sellers and buyers have legally binding documents that detail the legal requirements of the transactions.

The project procurement management processes are the following:

- **Plan Procurement**—The purpose of this process is to plan purchases, acquisitions, and the type of contracts to be used for transaction. The following are the steps to be taken during plan procurement:
    - Make or buy decision. Make the product or services as part of the project. Decide on buy decision as part of the procurement process.
    - Plan and decide on how much to buy.
    - When to buy the product and services. Timely purchase.
    - Decide on the type of contract (how much control do you want on the project procurement process):
    - Fixed Price Contract
        - Firm Fixed Price
        - Fixed Price Incentive Fee (FPIF)
        - Fixed Price Economic Price Adjustment (FP-EPA)
            - Time and Material
            - Cost Reimbursable Contracts
        - Cost Plus Fixed Fee (CPFF)
        - Cost Plus Incentive Fee (CPIF)
    - Plan the details of the selected contract.

- Prepare for Request for Proposal (RFP)/Request for Information (RFI)/Request for Quotation (RFQ).
- Define the scope of the proposal.
- No ambiguity in the contract details.
  - Create Statement of Work (SOW) for the product or service to be purchased.
  - Create selection criteria for the vendors to be selected.
- **Conduct Procurement**—This is the process that executes the activities defined in the procurement management plan. The procurement management plan can be found in the project management plan. The following are the activities to be executed during the conduct procurement process:
  - Qualified sellers must be in the organization procurement system. Evaluate only the qualifying vendors in the system.
  - Conduct bidders' conference.
  - Issue request to qualified vendors.
  - Evaluate seller proposals based on available resources such as experts and independent research of expected proposal content.
  - Request sellers response.
  - Evaluate responses.
  - Use the evaluation sheet.
  - Multiple evaluators.
  - Technical requirement (best).
  - Financial requirements (best).
  - Reference.
  - Rank the vendors.
    - Produce the final contract.
  - Legal documentation—Engage the legal department for the terms and conditions defined in the contract.
  - The project manager must look closely into the scope statements, functions—all that is needed to support the project and as defined in the SOW.
    - Award contract. Award the contract to the most qualified vendor as determined from the proposal evaluation.
- **Administer Procurement**—This is the management of contracts between the buyer and seller to ensure that the content agreed upon in the contract is delivered according to the terms defined in

the contract. Administrative activities during this process include the following:

- ○ Management of contract compliance.
  - Terms and conditions of the contract must not be violated.
  - Monitor the terms and conditions of the project.
  - Monitor term changes.
- ○ Payments systems.
  - To ensure that amount paid is as defined in the contract.
  - To ensure that payment is paid per the schedule defined in the contract.
  - The term and conditions of payment must be followed.
- ○ Change management and control of the contract contents.
  - A change management process must be in place to change the contract.
  - Any deviation from terms and conditions must be managed in the contract.
  - Manage to the exact terms of the contract.
- ○ Manage project performance with respect to the expectations defined in the contract.

- **Close Procurement**
  - ○ Final Acceptance—This is putting closure the procurement process by accepting the goods and services delivered if contract terms and conditions are acceptable.
  - ○ Release of final payment.
  - ○ Return of any property between the buyer and the seller.
  - ○ Gather lessons learned from working with the vendors.

Chapter 19: PMI Code of Ethics and Professional Conduct

This area of PMI standard is an important aspect that differentiates project managers as professional and nonprofessionals. A professional approach is applied to all situations irrespective of the circumstance surrounding the situations. The requirement from PMI standards is responsibility, respect, fairness, and honesty. My formula for memorizing this requirement is R²FH. The following sections of this book are copied directly from the PMI standard to avoid any misinterpretation and maintain accuracy as defined by Project Management Institute.

Source: PMP Handbook from PMI

PMI CHAPTER 1. VISION AND APPLICABILITY

1.1 Vision and Purpose

As practitioners of project management, we are committed to doing what is right and honorable. We set high standards for ourselves and we aspire to meet these standards in all aspects of our lives—at work, at home, and in service to our profession.

This Code of Ethics and Professional Conduct describes the expectations that we have of ourselves and our fellow practitioners in the global project management community. It articulates the ideals to which we aspire as well as the behaviors that are mandatory in our professional and volunteer roles.

The purpose of this Code is to instill confidence in the project management profession and to help an individual become a better practitioner. We do this by establishing a profession-wide understanding of appropriate behavior.

We believe that the credibility and reputation of the project management profession is shaped by the collective conduct of individual practitioners.

We believe that we can advance our profession, both individually and collectively, by embracing this Code of Ethics and Professional Conduct. We also believe that this Code will assist us in making wise decisions, particularly when faced with difficult situations where we may be asked to compromise our integrity or our values.

Our hope that this Code of Ethics and Professional Conduct will serve as a catalyst for others to study, deliberate, and write about ethics and values. Further, we hope that this Code will ultimately be used to build upon and evolve our profession.

1.2 Persons to Whom the Code Applies

The Code of Ethics and Professional Conduct applies to:
1.2.1 All PMI members
1.2.2 Individuals who are not members of PMI but meet one or more of the following criteria:
1. Non-members who hold a PMI certification
2. Non-members who apply to commence a PMI certification process
3. Non-members who serve PMI in a volunteer capacity.

Comment: *Those holding a Project Management Institute (PMI®) credential (whether members or not) were previously held accountable to the Project Management Professional (PMP®) or Certified Associate in Project Management (CAPM®) Code of Professional Conduct and continue to be held accountable to the PMI Code of Ethics and Professional Conduct. In the past, PMI also had separate ethics standards for members and for credentialed individuals. Stakeholders who contributed input to develop this Code concluded that having multiple codes was undesirable and that everyone should be held to one high standard. Therefore, this Code is applicable to both PMI members and individuals who have applied for or received a credential from PMI, regardless of their membership in PMI.*

1.3 Structure of the Code

The Code of Ethics and Professional Conduct is divided into sections that contain standards of conduct which are aligned with the four values that were identified as most important to the project management community. Some sections of this Code include comments. Comments are not mandatory parts of the Code, but provide examples and other clarification. Finally, a glossary can be found at the end of the standard. The glossary defines words and phrases used in the Code. For convenience, those terms defined in the glossary are underlined in the text of the Code.

1.4 Values that Support this Code

Practitioners from the global project management community were asked to identify the values that formed the basis of their decision making and guided their actions. The values that the global project management community defined as most important were: responsibility, respect, fairness, and honesty. This Code affirms these four values as its foundation.

1.5 Aspirational and Mandatory Conduct

Each section of the Code of Ethics and Professional Conduct includes both aspirational standards and mandatory standards. The aspirational standards describe the conduct that we strive to uphold as practitioners. Although adherence to the aspirational standards is not easily measured, conducting ourselves in accordance with these is an expectation that we have of ourselves as professionals—it is not optional. The mandatory standards establish firm requirements, and in some cases, limit or prohibit practitioner behavior. Practitioners who do not conduct themselves in accordance with these standards will be subject to disciplinary procedures before PMI's Ethics Review Committee.

Comment: *The conduct covered under the aspirational standards and conduct covered under the mandatory standards are not mutually exclusive; that is, one specific act or omission could violate both aspirational and mandatory standards.*

PMI CHAPTER 2. RESPONSIBILITY

2.1 Description of Responsibility

Responsibility is our duty to take ownership for the decisions we make or fail to make, the actions we take or fail to take, and the consequences that result.

2.2 Responsibility: Aspirational Standards

As practitioners in the global project management community:
> 2.2.1 We make decisions and take actions based on the best interests of society, public safety, and the environment.
> 2.2.2 We accept only those assignments that are consistent with our background, experience, skills, and qualifications.

Comment: *Where developmental or stretch assignments are being considered, we ensure that key stakeholders receive timely and complete information regarding the gaps in our qualifications so that they may make informed decisions regarding our suitability for a particular assignment. In the case of a contracting arrangement, we only bid on work that our organization is qualified to perform and we assign only qualified individuals to perform the work.*

> 2.2.3 We fulfill the commitments that we undertake—we do what we say we will do.
> 2.2.4 When we make errors or omissions, we take ownership and make corrections promptly. When we discover errors or omissions caused by others, we communicate them to the appropriate body as soon they are discovered. We accept accountability for any issues resulting from our errors or omissions and any resulting consequences.
> 2.2.5 We protect proprietary or confidential information that has been entrusted to us.
> 2.2.6 We uphold this Code and hold each other accountable to it.

2.3 Responsibility: Mandatory Standards

As practitioners in the global project management community, we require the following of ourselves and our fellow practitioners:

Regulations and Legal Requirements

2.3.1 We inform ourselves and uphold the policies, rules, regulations and laws that govern our work, professional, and volunteer activities.

2.3.2 We report unethical or illegal conduct to appropriate management and, if necessary, to those affected by the conduct.

Comment: *These provisions have several implications. Specifically, we do not engage in any illegal behavior, including but not limited to: theft, fraud, corruption, embezzlement, or bribery. Further, we do not take or abuse the property of others, including intellectual property, nor do we engage in slander or libel. In focus groups conducted with practitioners around the globe, these types of illegal behaviors were mentioned as being problematic. As practitioners and representatives of our profession, we do not condone or assist others in engaging in illegal behavior. We report any illegal or unethical conduct. Reporting is not easy and we recognize that it may have negative consequences. Since recent corporate scandals, many organizations have adopted policies to protect employees who reveal the truth about illegal or unethical activities. Some governments have also adopted legislation to protect employees who come forward with the truth.*

Ethics Complaints

2.3.3 We bring violations of this Code to the attention of the appropriate body for resolution.

2.3.4 We only file ethics complaints when they are substantiated by facts.

Comment: *These provisions have several implications. We cooperate with PMI concerning ethics violations and the collection of related information whether we are a complainant or a respondent. We also abstain from accusing others of ethical misconduct when we do not have all the facts. Further, we pursue disciplinary action against individuals who knowingly make false allegations against others.*

2.3.5 We pursue disciplinary action against an individual who retaliates against a person raising ethics concerns.

PMI CHAPTER 3. RESPECT

3.1 Description of Respect

Respect is our duty to show a high regard for ourselves, others, and the resources entrusted to us. Resources entrusted to us may include people, money, reputation, the safety of others, and natural or environmental resources.

An environment of respect engenders trust, confidence, and performance excellence by fostering mutual cooperation—an environment where diverse perspectives and views are encouraged and valued.

3.2 Respect: Aspirational Standards

As practitioners in the global project management community:
> 3.2.1 We inform ourselves about the norms and customs of others and avoid engaging in behaviors they might consider disrespectful.
> 3.2.2 We listen to others' points of view, seeking to understand them.
> 3.2.3 We approach directly those persons with whom we have a conflict or disagreement.
> 3.2.4 We conduct ourselves in a professional manner, even when it is not reciprocated.

Comment: *An implication of these provisions is that we avoid engaging in gossip and avoid making negative remarks to undermine another person's reputation. We also have a duty under this Code to confront others who engage in these types of behaviors.*

3.3 Respect: Mandatory Standards

As practitioners in the global project management community, we require the following of ourselves and our fellow practitioners:
> 3.3.1 We negotiate in good faith.
> 3.3.2 We do not exercise the power of our expertise or position to influence the decisions or actions of others in order to benefit personally at their expense.
> 3.3.3 We do not act in an abusive manner toward others.
> 3.3.4 We respect the property rights of others.

PMI CHAPTER 4. FAIRNESS

4.1 Description of Fairness

Fairness is our duty to make decisions and act impartially and objectively. Our conduct must be free from competing self interest, prejudice, and favoritism.

4.2 Fairness: Aspirational Standards

As practitioners in the global project management community:

4.2.1 We demonstrate transparency in our decision-making process.

4.2.2 We constantly reexamine our impartiality and objectivity, taking corrective action as appropriate.

Comment: *Research with practitioners indicated that the subject of conflicts of interest is one of the most challenging faced by our profession. One of the biggest problems practitioners report is not recognizing when we have conflicted loyalties and recognizing when we are inadvertently placing ourselves or others in a conflict of interest situation. We as practitioners must proactively search for potential conflicts and help each other by highlighting each other's potential conflicts of interest and insisting that they be resolved.*

4.2.3 We provide equal access to information to those who are authorized to have that information.

4.2.4 We make opportunities equally available to qualified candidates.

Comment: *An implication of these provisions is, in the case of a contracting arrangement, we provide equal access to information during the bidding process.*

4.3 Fairness: Mandatory Standards

As practitioners in the global project management community, we require the following of ourselves and our fellow practitioners:

Conflict of Interest Situations

4.3.1 We proactively and fully disclose any real or potential conflicts of interest to the appropriate stakeholders.

4.3.2 When we realize that we have a real or potential conflict of interest, we refrain from engaging in the decision-making process or otherwise attempting to influence outcomes, unless or until: we have made full disclosure to the affected stakeholders; we have an approved mitigation plan; and we have obtained the consent of the stakeholders to proceed.

Comment: *A conflict of interest occurs when we are in a position to influence decisions or other outcomes on behalf of one party when such decisions or outcomes could affect one or more other parties with which we have competing loyalties. For example, when we are acting as an employee, we have a duty of loyalty to our employer. When we are acting as a PMI volunteer, we have a duty of loyalty to the Project Management Institute. We must recognize these divergent interests and refrain from influencing decisions when we have a conflict of interest.*

Further, even if we believe that we can set aside our divided loyalties and make decisions impartially, we treat the appearance of a conflict of interest as a conflict of interest and follow the provisions described in the Code.

Favoritism and Discrimination

4.3.3 We do not hire or fire, reward or punish, or award or deny contracts based on personal considerations, including but not limited to, favoritism, nepotism, or bribery.

4.3.4 We do not discriminate against others based on, but not limited to, gender, race, age, religion, disability, nationality, or sexual orientation.

4.3.5 We apply the rules of the organization (employer, Project Management Institute, or other group) without favoritism or prejudice.

PMI CHAPTER 5. HONESTY

5.1 Description of Honesty

Honesty is our duty to understand the truth and act in a truthful manner both in our communications and in our conduct.

5.2 Honesty: Aspirational Standards

As practitioners in the global project management community:

5.2.1 We earnestly seek to understand the truth.

5.2.2 We are truthful in our communications and in our conduct.

5.2.3 We provide accurate information in a timely manner.

Comment: *An implication of these provisions is that we take appropriate steps to ensure that the information we are basing our decisions upon or providing to others is accurate, reliable, and timely. This includes having the courage to share bad news even when it may be poorly received. Also, when outcomes are negative, we avoid burying information or shifting blame to others. When outcomes are positive, we avoid taking credit for the achievements of others. These provisions reinforce our commitment to be both honest and responsible.*

5.2.4 We make commitments and promises, implied or explicit, in good faith.

5.2.5 We strive to create an environment in which others feel safe to tell the truth.

5.3 Honesty: Mandatory Standards

As practitioners in the global project management community, we require the following of ourselves and our fellow practitioners:

5.3.1 We do not engage in or condone behavior that is designed to deceive others, including but not limited to, making misleading or false statements, stating half-truths, providing information out of context or withholding information that, if known, would render our statements as misleading or incomplete.

5.3.2 We do not engage in dishonest behavior with the intention of personal gain or at the expense of another.

Comment: *The aspirational standards exhort us to be truthful. Half-truths and non-disclosures intended to mislead stakeholders are as unprofessional as affirmatively making misrepresentations. We develop credibility by providing complete and accurate information.*

APPENDIX A

A.1 History of this Standard

PMI's vision of project management as an independent profession drove our early work in ethics. In 1981, the PMI Board of Directors formed an Ethics, Standards and Accreditation Group. One task required the group to deliberate on the need for a code of ethics for the profession. The team's report contained the first documented PMI discussion of ethics for the project management profession. This report was submitted to the PMI Board of Directors in August 1982 and published as a supplement to the August 1983 Project Management Quarterly.

In the late 1980's, this standard evolved to become the Ethics Standard for the Project Management Professional [PMP®]. In 1997, the PMI Board determined the need for a member code of ethics. The PMI Board formed the Ethics Policy Documentation Committee to draft and publish an ethics standard for PMI's membership. The Board approved the new Member Code of Ethics in October 1998. This was followed by Board approval of the Member Case Procedures in January 1999, which provided a process for the submission of an ethics complaint and a determination as to whether a violation had occurred.

Since the 1998 Code was adopted, many dramatic changes have occurred within PMI and the business world. PMI membership has grown significantly. A great deal of growth has also occurred in regions outside North America. In the business world, ethics scandals have caused the downfall global corporations and non-profits, causing public outrage and sparking increased government regulations. Globalization has brought economies closer together but has caused a realization that our practice of ethics may differ from culture to culture. The rapid, continuing pace of technological change has provided new opportunities, but has also introduced new challenges, including new ethical dilemmas.

For these reasons, in 2003 the PMI Board of Directors called for the reexamination of our codes of ethics. In 2004, the PMI Board commissioned the Ethics Standards Review Committee [ESRC] to review the codes of ethics and develop a process for revising the codes. The ESRC developed processes that would encourage active participation by the global project management community. In 2005, the PMI Board approved the processes for revising the code, agreeing that global participation by the project management community was paramount. In 2005, the Board also commissioned the Ethics Standards Development Committee to carry out the Board-approved process and deliver the revised code by the end of 2006. This Code of Ethics and Professional Development was approved by the PMI Board of Directors in October 2006.

A.2 Process Used to Create This Standard

The first step by the Ethics Standards Development Committee [ESDC] in the development of this Code was to understand the ethical issues facing the project management community and to understand the values and viewpoints of practitioners from all regions of the globe. This was accomplished by a variety of mechanisms including focus group discussions and two internet surveys involving practitioners, members, volunteers, and people holding a PMI certification. Additionally, the team analyzed the ethics codes of 24 non-profit associations from various regions of the world, researched best practices in the development of ethics standards, and explored the ethics-related tenets of PMI's strategic plan.

This extensive research conducted by the ESDC provided the backdrop for developing the exposure draft of the PMI Code of Ethics and Professional Conduct. The exposure draft was circulated to the global project management community for comment. The rigorous, standards development processes established by the American National Standards Institute were followed during the development of the Code because these processes were used for PMI technical standard development projects and were deemed to represent the best practices for obtaining and adjudicating stakeholder feedback to the exposure draft.

The result of this effort is a Code of Ethics and Professional Conduct that not only describes the ethical values to which the global project management community aspires, but also addresses the specific conduct that is mandatory for every individual bound by this Code. Violations of the PMI Code of Ethics and Professional Conduct may result in sanctions by PMI under the ethics Case Procedures.

The ESDC learned that as practitioners of project management, our community takes its commitment to ethics very seriously and we hold ourselves and our peers in the global project management community accountable to conduct ourselves in accordance with the provisions of this Code.

APPENDIX B

B.1 Glossary

Abusive Manner. Conduct that results in physical harm or creates intense feelings of fear, humiliation, manipulation, or exploitation in another person.

Conflict of Interest. A situation that arises when a practitioner of project management is faced with making a decision or doing some act that will benefit the practitioner or another person or organization to which the practitioner owes a duty of loyalty and at the same time will harm another person or organization to which the practitioner owes a similar duty of loyalty. The only way practitioners can resolve conflicting duties is to disclose the conflict to those affected and allow them to make the decision about how the practitioner should proceed.

Duty of Loyalty. A person's responsibility, legal or moral, to promote the best interest of an organization or other person with whom they are affiliated.

Project Management Institute [PMI]. The totality of the Project Management Institute, including it's

Committees, groups, and chartered components such as chapters, colleges, and specific interest groups.

PMI Member. A person who has joined the Project Management Institute as a member.

PMI-Sponsored Activities. Activities that include, but are not limited to, participation on a PMI Member

Advisory Group, PMI standard development team, or another PMI working group or committee. This also includes activities engaged in under the auspices of a chartered PMI component organization—whether it is in a leadership role in the component or another type of component educational activity or event.

Practitioner. A person engaged in an activity that contributes to the management of a project, portfolio, or program, as part of the project management profession.

PMI Volunteer. A person who participates in PMI-sponsored activities, whether a member of the Project Management Institute or not.

About the Author

O. A. Amao, BEng (Hons), MEng (Hons), MIEE, PMP, from Coventry University, UK, is a principal consultant with big five consulting companies. He consulted for several Fortune 1000 clients worldwide including American Management Systems, UK; Capgemini; Ernst & Young, USA; Convergys, USA; Brown & Sharpe, UK; and British Gas, and now with AITechConsulting Ltd.

His experience includes business, engineering, and IT consultation for major corporations in countries including Great Britain, France, Spain, Germany, Switzerland, Saudi Arabia, and the USA. His experience in project and program management included project management of multidisciplinary large-scale billing and operation support systems for telecom, transportation, retail, financial, and manufacturing industries.

AITECHCONSULTING LLC, USA.

PO Box 1213
Laurel, MD, 20725, USA
Attention: General Counsel
Phone: 1 888-847-8824
Fax: 301-362-1125
E-mail: general.counsel@eazypmp.com
Website: www.eazypmp.com